D0622942

Knox-Johnston On Sailing

Robin Knox-Johnston

Registered Office
John Wiley & Sons Ltd, The Atrium, Southern Gate, Chichester, West Sussex, PO19 8SQ,
United Kingdom

Editorial Office
John Wiley & Sons Ltd, The Atrium, Southern Gate, Chichester, West Sussex, PO19 8SQ,
United Kingdom

For details of our global editorial offices, for customer services and for information about how to apply
for permission to reuse the copyright material in this book please see our website at www.wiley.com

The author would like to acknowledge the contribution of Belinda Bird as Editor, and Ben Davies as
Research Assistant.

Library of Congress Cataloging-in-Publication Data

Knox-Johnston, Robin.
  Knox-Johnston on sailing / Robin Knox-Johnston.
    p. cm.
  Includes bibliographical references and index.
  ISBN 978-0-470-97251-9 (hardback)
  1. Sailing.   I. Title.
  GV811.K718 2010
  797.1'24–dc22

                         2010028558

A catalogue record for this book is available from the British Library.

WILEY 🧭 NAUTICAL

Set in 12/14pt Garamond by Aptara Inc., New Delhi, India
Printed in Great Britain by TJ International Ltd, Padstow, Cornwall

CONTENTS

CONTENTS

CONTENTS

FOREWORD

Although, in theory, a magazine editor has a free hand over the content of their magazine, in practice major changes to the editorial mix are very difficult, though not impossible, to implement. In practice the only time the editor is free to perform major surgery is when they first take over. Such was my situation when I took over a faltering *Yachting World* in late 1992 and in I waded with a sharp axe. In fact so sharp was that axe that by the time I planned out my first issue as Editor there were only two out of several regular features left in the mix. One of those was Robin Knox-Johnston's regular column which continues today some 18 years later. In this Robin brings an uncommon dash of seamanship and common sense that keeps *Yachting World* bolted firmly to the floor as a foil to the hi-tech world of racing, the America's Cup and the latest technical wizardry.

Don't get me wrong. Robin, or Sir Robin as he is now, is far from being a dyed-in-the-wool traditionalist. His knowledge and writing spans everything from current ideas to the traditional as is well illustrated by the fact that he still sails his decidedly low-tech gaff ketch *Suhaili* despite racing the ultra high-tech Open 60 *Grey Power* in the last Velux 5 Oceans round the world solo race. What his column recognises and promotes is that there are many aspects of sailing and seagoing that are every bit as relevant today as they would have been a century ago.

The way we go to sea might change but the sea, and wind, remain the same.

What makes Robin so different from many other yachtsmen who have achieved great things is that having, in 1969, become the first person to sail solo, non-stop round the world, he continued to be very active in the sport with other circumnavigations and notable passages to his credit all without self-aggrandisement. Not only that, he remains even today, Britain's best-known sailor and promoter of sailing in its broadest sense. Which is why, in 1992, that sharp axe passed over his column. And let's hope he stays on as a *Yachting World* columnist for many years to come.

Andrew Bray
June 2010

PREFACE

The world of yachting has changed massively since I set sail on *Suhaili*, my 32ft ketch, to sail around the world. That was in 1968 and the voyage took 312 days at an average speed of just over four knots. As I write, the current solo record stands at just 57 days. I have been lucky enough to be involved with this transformation from tortoise to hare, competing on giant multihulls, round the buoys in the Admiral's Cup and on Open 60 monohulls – though *Suhaili* has stayed with me throughout.

Technology has transformed sailing. Composite materials, weather routing, self-steering systems and satellites – which have given us instant communications, weather information and global positioning – have allowed yachtsmen to sail faster and faster and the records will continue to fall. There is, however, more to sailing than battling the oceans and the record books. The thrill of exploration, whether of Greenland's frozen shores or of a quiet local creek, is something that every sailor feels, and it continues to draw me to the sea and provide a wide range of subjects for my *Yachting World* column.

Over the past 18 years writing for *Yachting World* each month has been a huge pleasure, and one I still enjoy, although sometimes the deadlines have crept up on me! I have been given a free rein, allowing me to change my focus from the latest race or rescue to more general reflections on sailing and seamanship. This selection reflects that diversity. I hope there is something here for everyone to enjoy.

Robin Knox-Johnston
June 2010

PART ONE

Going Places

THE DEVIL YOU KNOW

Every sailor thinks his own part of the world has the nastiest stretch of water. Robin thinks the Thames Estuary takes a lot of beating . . .

Have you noticed that wherever you sail in the world, with very few exceptions, the local yachtsmen will always tell you that they have the most dangerous sailing conditions anywhere on Earth?

My first introduction to this peculiarity came when sailing back from India a few decades ago. Before we left Bombay, we were warned about the dangers of the Indian Ocean. We miraculously survived the crossing to Muscat, to be told there that the coastline down to Aden was far more difficult. In Mombasa, the treacherous crossing of all these dangers was as nothing compared with the East African coast, and so on.

Wherever we arrived, people dismissed what we had been through, except, of course, the last day or two as we approached their area – where we had obviously been lucky.

We actually did believe them in East London when they told us about the Cape of Good Hope, but the Capetonians were much more in awe of the Skeleton Coast.

The people of Brest will tell you about the Chenal du Four, Australians about the Tasman, Hong Kong sailors about the China Sea.

Personally, I have always felt that the Thames Estuary takes some beating. An easterly gale on an ebb tide from Sea Reach onwards creates conditions which no one in their right mind would wish to experience in a small yacht.

However, I assumed that this was just my own prejudice until French sailor, Titouan Lamazou, told me that he was concerned at the possibility of bringing his 140ft sloop, drawing 6.5m, to London in 1993. He, like many other Frenchmen, found the estuary alarming, not because of the wind and waves, but on account of the banks and tides.

I am sympathetic. The Thames is not easy and the unwary can swiftly find themselves aground some distance from their DR position – especially now the number of navigation marks has been reduced. Even in moderate visibility I consider the Thames to be the complete justification for investing in GPS.

TOGETHER ACROSS
THE POND

Crossing the Atlantic is still a major achievement, no matter how many others have already done it. The Atlantic Rally for Cruisers is a good way for amateur sailors to cross in company.

I f John of Gaunt's grandsons had been interchanged so that King Henry V of England had been Prince Henry the Navigator of Portugal and vice versa, then it is just possible that England might have started exploring by sea earlier: any one of the Canary Islands, Madeira or the Azores might have been English, not Spanish or Portuguese.

Of course, we would not have had Agincourt, but as compensation there would have been a nice warm Atlantic island in the Northern Hemisphere, selling beer instead of wine. Whether this is a great loss is a moot point; a major attraction of the islands, in addition to the mild maritime climates, of course, is their Iberian charm.

Of the three, the Canary Islands might be said to have staked an early claim as the jumping off point for an Atlantic crossing, since Columbus sailed from Gomera, one of the group.

There was practical logic in this. The Azores are on the edge of the westerlies, usually in their grip during winter when they can reach storm force (I experienced 98 knots in December 1989 while moored in Praia da Vitoria), so a voyage west was likely to be against the wind in the winter and beset by calms in the summer.

In the days before proper salting of meat and no means of keeping water sweet, voyages were severely restricted to the length of time the available stores lasted.

Madeira is in the middle of the Horse Latitudes, between the westerlies and north-east trades, so lack of wind is more likely to be a problem for an Atlantic crossing from there. The Canary Islands are at the northern edge of the trade winds where a westerly passage can find variables in winter, but usually steady winds in summer.

This made the Canaries the perfect place of departure for the square-rigged vessels that dominated oceanic transport until just over 100 years ago. Latitude, and these following winds, provide another benefit from this route, sometimes called the southern route, which is an easy, warm voyage across to the West Indies – provided the hurricane season is avoided, of course.

Those factors are just as applicable today and make the Canary Islands an ideal starting point for the Atlantic Rally for Cruisers, now known as the ARC.

Ocean cruising can trace its roots back more than 140 years, but even as recently as 1960 a transatlantic voyage was rare and seen as something special. Since then, yachting has had a huge increase in popularity. Inevitably, as people have become more experienced and adventurous and have had more leisure time, they have wanted to explore further.

There are no figures for the number of yachts crossing the Atlantic, but it must be into the thousands each year. Not all skippers are highly experienced – indeed, some are making the voyage just in order to gain experience and this is where the ARC concept is so beneficial.

The sea is never going to be a safe place, but a number of yachts sailing together does provide some security. This is the ultimate secret of the event, because it helps allay the fears of most amateur crews.

Radio allows the boats instant contact, so although they might not sight another entrant after the start, there is no need to feel alone. Each boat knows that another must be only a few hours away, to offer assistance in an emergency. There are advantages, too, in such groups sailing, as *Notices to Mariners* can be issued advising commercial vessels to be more watchful.

The ARC is the antithesis of such events as the America's Cup and the Whitbread Round the World Race since it is an event for the amateur. Although there is a mild competitive element, the prime reason for entering is, I suspect, the company. The number of entries indicates the popularity of the concept.

In 1986, when the first ARC was organised, a total of 204 yachts took part, still a record for a transoceanic race and a clear indication that it fulfilled a need. The lowest entry was 97 in 1993, but by 2009 they had more than 200.

SCOTLAND THE
MAGNIFICENT

A safe anchorage surrounded by empty mountains is Robin's idea of satisfying cruising. He found it in the Arctic, but you don't have to go so far to find clear night skies, sparsely populated anchorages and the grandeur of a mountain backdrop.

N
ext to racing, I think the most satisfying aspect of sailing must come from approaching a new coastline. There are the heightened senses as you navigate into a previously unknown area and the anticipation of a fresh port or anchorage to explore.

If the area is uninhabited, so much the better, as it then provides those increasingly rare commodities – privacy and freedom from social constraints.

Moored in a safe anchorage, surrounded by clean, untouched and empty mountains or hills brings a contentment that is hard to equal. There are not many places left in Europe where this is possible, which is why the Arctic is so attractive.

A recent excuse to go to the north-west of Scotland showed me that it is not necessary to travel so far to find the same grandeur! True, there are more boats about and the chances of being sole occupant of a loch are less, but the coast has been heavily indented over the centuries and there is a wide choice of lochs.

Usually there is no need to anchor within miles of another yacht. The mountains are higher in Greenland, of course, and glaciers are not to be found in Scotland, but the land has that greater ruggedness that comes from less weathering.

The head of a loch is likely to be inhabited by sheep on bright green grass rather than the barren gravel and occasional scrub at the head of a fjord, but this is only due to a few degrees' difference in temperature and the effect of time.

From the sailor's point of view, when searching for a good anchorage, the water close to the head of a loch is likely to shoal more gradually, not abruptly as is common further north. This has the drawback that the anchor will probably have to be laid further out, but there is less risk of dragging into deeper water or swinging into the steep edge of recently deposited silt, so often the case in Arctic fjords.

Anyone listening to the weather forecasts could be excused from gaining the impression that Scotland was the subject of continual high winds and constant heavy rainfall. Both occur, but generally less in summer when the Atlantic depressions track further north.

There is a benefit in being closer to the depression's paths, though, as the weather changes more quickly so that if it is unpleasant today, one can be confident that it will be better tomorrow. In most cases, if not tucked into one of the small coves that are to be found from careful examination of the charts, the worst of the bad weather can be avoided by shifting a few miles to a new lee as the wind changes.

It is said that in the British Isles we have weather, not a climate, but this is what gives us the wonderful variety and changes in colour and this is a particularly attractive feature of Scotland's west coast.

May is often a very good month in Scotland as the weather has improved and the midges have not yet expanded their numbers to the point that they make Dracula seem like an amateur at drawing blood.

Head nets and shirts that cover all exposed flesh are advisable, but these won't keep out all of them and an insect-repelling cream is an essential part of the yacht's stores. Smoke will drive some away, coils are effective. Closing all the hatches works to a point, but the sight of midges collected round the hatch, yearning for access to your skin, can be unnerving.

The best measure is to anchor at least 200 metres from the nearest land if this is possible. Even there the odd marathon midge will reach you.

If this all sounds as if paradise has nettles – well, that's no bad thing. The west coast of Scotland is one of the cruising yachtsman's best-kept secrets and we don't want it becoming overcrowded!

ANY PLANS FOR THE SUMMER?

Planning the summer cruise can be a question of compromise, especially if your other half is not keen on long passages. In June 2005 Robin was looking forward to his own summer venture – to the east coast of Greenland.

Have you planned your summer cruise? Assuming you are not spending a season racing round the cans, the annual question of where to cruise presents yachtsmen with a wide range of choices. The decision usually comes down to available time. How long can the crew afford to be away? How far can their boat reasonably expect to go and return and leave enough time to spend at the chosen destination?

It seems to me we have had more days with easterly winds in recent years, which makes going westwards easier. But, of course, you still have to return, and in any case you cannot order ideal weather in advance, so there has to be time built into a schedule for unfavourable conditions or beating, an issue which becomes more of a priority as Monday in the office looms ever closer.

A long beat might also be a disincentive to less enthusiastic female members of the family. My observation has indicated most men sail despite their wives (not to spite them, note!) and what intelligent woman would give up a stable, dry, well-ordered home where everything stays where you put it and she can get a full night's uninterrupted sleep for a heaving, rolling, pitching, damp one, with limited storage space and which demands anti-social hours of service? (That 35% of Clipper crews are female goes some way to disprove this point.)

My wife always suffered from seasickness for the first couple of days of sailing, although she crossed the Atlantic with me twice and did thousands of miles of quietish cruising. Nor did she find her sea legs as we got older – indeed, she was taking longer to get over seasickness – so our plans for distant cruising during retirement were changed to my doing ocean crossings alone or with non-seasick friends and she would fly over to join us for the coastal cruising.

For an average cruiser based on the UK south coast, a cruise to the west coast of Ireland or Scotland may be a bit far unless the boat can be pre-positioned closer to the destination.

Size makes a difference, of course. Larger boats travel faster and their size means waves are relatively smaller, plus they provide more space below, so living during longer cruises is more organised. But while they expand the potential range, larger boats cost more to buy, berth and maintain. Draught will be a consideration, too.

My plans for this summer involve a certain amount of pre-positioning a large yacht and one of the most fascinating places I know as the final destination – the east coast of Greenland. The boat will sail to Reykjavik, where I join it. We then plan to go down to Cape Farvel and get behind the ice that screens the east coast until July. It disperses from the south coast so the south-west and west coasts are usually clear, which explains why the Viking settlements were in this area. As and when the ice clears on the east coast we plan to move up the coast towards Scoresby Sund.

On the way I am going to drop off at Kangerlussuaq because Chris Bonington and I have some unfinished business with the Cathedral

Mountain. We thought we had reached the summit 14 years ago, only to discover there was a peak slightly higher nearby, but separated by a deep ravine. Oncoming snow forced us back down and we ran out of time for another attempt.

The whole plan is ice-dependent, of course. No season is exactly the same as the previous one and the ice that streams down the coast, varying in extent from 2 to 20 miles, may or may not be there – we have no idea how global warming is affecting it, but seven years ago the ice was 20 miles deep off Angmassalik, which we reached with some difficulty.

It is possible to force a yacht through and hope that the fjords inside are less congested, provided there is no risk of strong winds that can move the ice before them at quite astonishing speeds. The floes will move if you push gently against them, but if they start to get compressed by the wind then a yacht should be well clear.

These fjords are usually relatively ice-free if no glaciers descend into them, but this becomes less likely as you move further north.

MEAT SOUP IN ICELAND

Thwarted by thick ice off Greenland in 2005, Robin and climber Chris Bonington curtailed a planned cruise and returned to Iceland to luxuriate in saunas, strap on the crampons and help out with a song during Meat Soup Night.

The ice off East Greenland in August this year extended to 100 miles from the coast, blocking access to Angmassalik and Kangerlussuaq, the intended destination for Chris Bonington and me aboard *Antiope*. So, we headed to Iceland instead. The north-west corner looked promising, with a group of fjords rotating out of the main entrant named Isafjardardjup and an ice cap not far from the fjords to provide a climbing interest.

We re-entered Iceland at Isafjordur, a small, very protected port on the south side of the group, and berthed between trawlers. Fishing is the town's lifeblood, but with cod catches being limited to 200,000 tons a year to keep stocks stable, a dramatic fall from 30 years ago when the annual catch could be maintained at 500,000 tons, the large stern trawlers spend a lot of their time in port. Cruise liners visit in summer, but the larger ones have to anchor outside the port.

Like all Icelandic towns, it is scrupulously clean, but there is not much to see apart from the fish wharves and an excellent museum. For us, its public baths were attraction enough; the sensation of cleanliness from a shower and sauna was as good as any cultural attraction.

Local mountaineers and sailors quickly came down to see what we planned (and look over the boat) and mentioned that if we wanted to cross a northern fjord called Hesteyrarjordur, we could anchor and join a large party gathered for something unpronounceable that roughly translated into Meat Soup Night.

How could we refuse that? So, over we went, motoring alongside a large humpback whale in the main fjord on the way. We anchored a cable offshore in 6m of water and dinghied ashore to join more than 100 people gathered in the largest of a small group of summer houses.

The main purpose of the meeting was to enjoy a communal meal of what can best be described as Irish stew, adding credence to the claim that the Irish arrived in Iceland long before the Vikings. This was followed by a singsong around a raging fire on the beach. For the British contribution, we provided *Molly Malone* and *Drunken Sailor*, whose choruses proved popular.

We returned on board in relays throughout the night and the next morning cruised round to a neighbouring fjord, Hrafnsfjordur, where we anchored in 6m near the inner end. Like so many fjords, there was a shoaling patch at the entrance and this one shallowed to 7m where a glacier had deposited the crushed rock and soil it had brought to its outlet. But the fjord deepened to more than 20m once this was passed, then slowly shoaled towards its upper end.

These Icelandic fjords were seldom more than 60m deep in the centre and shoaled at the sides, whereas in Greenland their depth was often around 600m and steep at the sides. Anchoring in Iceland is much easier as a result and the holding is usually good with a CQR.

We were now close to the north-west Iceland ice cap and decided to get to its summit. The evening was spent preparing climbing equipment and at 0400 we landed and climbed up through grass that slowly turned to rough rock, steeper and riddled with streams as the ice cap neared.

The rock supports an amazing variety of tiny flowers and some equally small butterflies, but fortunately none of the midges that would be found in Scotland or southern Greenland.

Once on the ice we donned crampons and roped up, then made our way past the inevitable crevasses to where the ice levelled out until, in thick mist and only thanks to GPS, we found ourselves at 2,905ft. Sadly, we had reached the summit, so we failed to achieve a Munro by 95ft!

The effort of tramping 23 miles in 14 hours sated the hunger for further mountains and with low pressure systems beginning to creep eastwards around Cape Farvel, we decided to head for home. Northern Iceland is lovely in summer, but once winter gales begin to arrive it is not an enjoyable place for yachting.

Frustratingly, September was reported to be the most ice-free month in Greenland this year. Next time, perhaps.

THE BANE OF BISCAY

Its reputation precedes it – and is not always deserved – but there are many reasons why the Bay of Biscay is such a tricky obstacle for those sailing away from British shores.

The Bay of Biscay is a permanent obstacle we cannot avoid for sailing vessels heading west or south away from the British Isles. Its reputation gives the impression that the weather is more severe there than, say, the English Channel, but in practice this is not the case.

A storm that comes into the Bay, as we had at the beginning of the Velux 5 Oceans race in October 2006, will come north to the United Kingdom. The waves built up by the wind are the result of the depressions that run over the British Isles and these affect the Bay in the same way, although often the wind decreases the further south you go.

The long Atlantic swell shortens in the Channel and the eastern part of the Bay as the floor of the Atlantic rises and the waves become steeper

17

when you reach soundings, historically at a depth of 200 fathoms. You can often feel and see the change as you pass over this contour.

Biscay is as open to the prevailing south-westerly gales as the Channel, so why has it got such a reputation?

The main reason is its size. From Ushant to Cape Vilano, which marks the southern end of the Bay rather than Cape Finisterre, is 360 miles in a south-westerly to southerly direction. In the days of sailing ships, and for many yachts, it can be a three to six-day passage and the chances that a gale might come through in that period are quite high – and much more so in the winter.

If you allow a couple of days to get to the beginning at Ushant, then the chances of meeting a gale are even higher. The problem is that the gale is almost certainly going to be a south-westerly, probably the direction you are trying to go, forcing a long and uncomfortable beat and, perhaps, the need to heave to before a welcome front comes through and, after a sharp increase in wind strength accompanied by rain, veers the wind round to the west or north-west and it becomes possible to free off for Finisterre.

You can get lucky and get a north-west round to easterly wind. Traditionally, this is what you wait for if you are setting off to break round the world records so you get clear of the Bay as speedily as possible. In the case of *ENZA New Zealand* in 1994, waiting for the right conditions enabled us to round Finisterre in just 19 hours. There the wind became the traditional Nortada off the Portuguese coast, which allowed a three-day run to the Canary Islands. Against this, it took seven days in *Suhaili* in 1968 and five days in 2001, including a period hove-to.

My first experience of the Bay was as a first tripper on a cargo ship. The conditions were not too bad, probably about Force 6, and this is the first and last time I have ever been seasick. Nine months later, coming back across the Bay in a storm, I was forward lookout, stuck right forward behind the bulwark at the prow. The ship was pitching heavily, sending fountains of water through the hawspipes behind me. It was awesome and wonderful.

When my relief was due, he failed to arrive and, after 30 minutes, I rang five bells to tell the bridge I had not been relieved. An Aldis light flashed from the bridge signalling me to report back there. I ran the gauntlet of the waves on the foredeck and climbed up the bridge to find it full of activity. An SOS had been received from the German sail-training ship *Pamir*. We were not asked to go to her assistance, being too far away. She sank with the loss of all but eight of her crew.

The old rule for square riggers was that when the wind was south-westerly, you headed west and if the wind direction did not change, you kept a westerly course until you could go on to the starboard tack and on that tack sail west of Finisterre. Of course, square riggers could only sail to within six points of the wind, nearly 70°, whereas a modern yacht can do better.

Sometimes it does not do very much better though, especially if the wind is strong, as then leeway will increase. This was a sensible practice as, if you tack into the Bay of Biscay and something goes wrong, there are not many easy places to seek shelter and from Ushant to Biarritz is a 360-mile-long lee shore.

IT'S NOT CRICKET!

The wicket was a little suspect, and the scoring certainly was, but the annual Brambles Bank cricket match in the middle of the Solent is all part of Britain's yachting tradition, says Robin.

We arrived off the pitch at 0520 in August 2009. The Solent was calm and deserted. I edged gingerly towards the Brambles Bank, cut the engine and waited. Half an hour later lights began to close in on us as the other players and spectators arrived. At 0600 small breakers began to appear and then the bank emerged.

We waited.

Within half an hour a sizeable section of the Brambles Bank was exposed, stretching from the Beacon north and west. There were two choices, the eastern bank next to the Beacon, and 150m to the west a reserve pitch had also appeared. The officials went ashore and declared the eastern pitch fit for the annual Brambles Cricket Match between the Royal Southern Yacht Club and the Island Sailing Club.

The surface of the Brambles Bank was good sand, but pockmarked with a series of pools, some as much as two feet deep. At each end of the pitch pools were right in the way of a sensible run up, and there were two more along the wicket. It would have taken an Olympic triple jump medallist to have bowled fast, and clearly spin was not an option. I could not see how anything less than a full toss had any chance of even reaching the batsman.

To my inexperienced eye the pitch required a very heavy roller – in fact, a bulldozer might not have gone amiss. But I said nothing. I had never seen the match before and was unsure what traditions had developed since the 1920s when Uffa Fox first organised it.

The veterans seemed totally unfazed by the state of the ground. Perhaps it is like this every year, I don't know, but I put on a nonchalant air as if I had expected nothing else. After all, Colin Cowdray had played here and if he thought it was alright, who was I to disagree?

The captains tossed, the Island would bat first and, after a quick assessment of the tide, eight overs a side were agreed.

Play was called. Our bowler stepped gingerly round a pool and flung the ball down. It thudded into the sand a yard short of the batsman and stayed put. The pitch was still a bit wet. The cry of "*Bowling Shane*" went up. Although I am not sure of the significance, I am aware of the provenance. A couple of runs were scored and it was Over.

The second ball of the second over came straight towards me. I ran forward to take an easy catch, but then my instincts took control. I missed the catch by a foot, but had I caught it I would have fallen headlong into a pool. I bowled next. Two full tosses were dispatched to the boundary, a variable perimeter which depended on the rate the tide moved in or out, and signalled not very gallantly by the umpire as sixes.

My next two balls thudded into the far side of a pool roughly between me and the batsman, leaving him expectant, but baffled. But at least I had discovered how to keep the run rate down.

At the end of the eight overs the Island Sailing Club had amassed a total of about 28 by my count – it was hard to tell, because the scoreboard was not always in tune with what was going on in the game and showed 180.

Our first batsman just about won the game for us. I scored two or perhaps three, about the average I have maintained for 40 years. Geoff Holt scored more than me, even though he required a runner, as moving him in his wheelchair from one end to the other needed a team of strong men on that surface.

The Royal Southern won with a questionable 738 runs. Apparently it was their turn, yet another cricket puzzle for a non-Englishman to comprehend. The tide was returning fast, boundaries were becoming easier, so stumps were drawn and we got back in our boats and repaired to the Royal Southern for an excellent breakfast.

It was not an international – 100 miles away a much more serious match was taking place at the Oval where England were on their way to winning the Ashes against Australia. But cricket, which might be described as England's civilising gift to the world, has been played on strange pitches on all five continents and this match is part of yachting tradition.

PART TWO

Sailing Solo

SUHAILI RETIRES

Once described as a tortoise among hares, *Suhaili* proved her worth as a survivor on her historic voyage round the world in 1969. Putting her into the National Maritime Museum in 1998 felt to Robin like sending a close relative into a home . . .

Exhibiting *Suhaili* in the new hall at the National Maritime Museum made me feel that I had just put a close relative into an old people's home. Since 1963 she has dominated my life, got me out of situations I should never have got into and been a loyal companion in some wonderful adventures.

'Workmanlike' is how she has often been described and I have never found that insulting. She is a workmanlike little boat. Her timbers – teak, all seven tons of it – are as strong as when we first put her together years ago in Bombay.

Sturdy, simple, she is based upon Colin Archer's inimitable designs for the Norwegian sailing lifeboats, the classic shape for a seaworthy family ocean cruiser. To the uninitiated she looks nothing in particular, just another yacht, a bit old-fashioned with her long keel and stout sternpost supporting the rudder, the propeller sticking out like an afterthought.

This is no Formula One racing machine, no ocean greyhound; this is a bulldog, a stayer, a boat that can stubbornly continue towards her objective, regardless of all going on around her.

She can never be glamorous, but, unlike most, she will always occupy her small place in maritime history. She holds a record that cannot be broken. She is the first vessel to sail non-stop round the world.

When we found ourselves a part of *The Sunday Times* Golden Globe race back in 1968, *Suhaili* was described as the tortoise among hares. It was not an unreasonable description. She was not built to survive the Southern Ocean; she was not built for speed; she was not a special purchase for the event.

Suhaili was what I had, and since I could find no sponsorship, what I had to accept if I wanted to participate. It was one of the best decisions of my life.

More stoutly built than all the others, simple to maintain, easy to repair, but above all, once I had learnt how to set her for up it, a magnificent survivor in the maelstrom of the Southern Ocean.

We could not outrun the waves, as can a modern multihull or Whitbread 60; *Suhaili* at ten tons is the same weight as the 92ft *ENZA New Zealand* [in which Robin broke another world record in 1994] so we had to heave to, warps trailing astern to provide a restraint against the surges down huge waves that can so often lead to a fatal broach.

Our average speed, even in those strong wind conditions, seldom exceeded 5.5 knots and we laboriously ground down the longitude from the Cape of Good Hope to Cape Horn in five months of cold, exposed sailing, when oilskins did not keep out the water so clothing was seldom dry. But thrown about, knocked down, washed over by huge waves, she bobbed up and kept plugging along.

Someone once said of *Suhaili* that she proved that anyone could get her round the world and they were right. Provided I kept faith in her, she showed she could do it.

So why put her away in a concrete pit in Greenwich? The answers are complex. As a Trustee I was aware that the museum needed a yacht as part of the display area it is creating beneath a glass roof over the West Wing courtyard. Of course, there are modern boats which might have done, but we need to teach the young that they don't have to have the latest equipment to succeed; simple gear might be the better bet.

But besides all this, I was beginning to worry about *Suhaili's* fastenings, the only part of her showing signs of decay. She is massively over-fastened – two bolts per strake per frame – some of which we have renewed. But the bulk are still holding so well, even if they display surface rust, that removing one might lead to a cracked frame.

Nevertheless, if I am to contemplate any more long voyages, she really ought to be refastened, so leaving her at Greenwich for a few years will allow the original steel bolts to corrode a little and make their removal simpler.[1]

She is only on loan, after all.

---

[1] Note: *Suhaili* was removed from the National Maritime Museum in 2002 and was refastened by the Elephant Boatyard in Burseldon. Robin still owns her and he sailed her up the Thames in April 2009 to celebrate the 40th anniversary of his groundbreaking circumnavigation.

30 YEARS ON

On the 30th anniversary of the completion of his round the world solo exploit, Robin reflects on the changes in the equipment available to the solo sailor.

O n 22 April 1999, it was exactly 30 years since *Suhaili* sailed back into Falmouth at the end of her 312-day non-stop circumnavigation. She looked worn, her sails were stained and by then mostly hand-sewn, and the self-steering had gone finally near Australia. None of the electrics worked, but this hardly mattered as there were no instruments to fail anyway, except a Walker log.

Suhaili was still in one piece, though; her rig was intact and had required only one replacement during the voyage – and none to the standing rigging. I was physically stronger than I had ever been, before or since.

My only worry, a really big one at the time, was how I had managed mentally. Apart from a short chat with some fishermen off New

Zealand, I had not spoken to anyone for ten and a half months. I'd had no one to compare myself with.

Although only five years old at that time, *Suhaili* was not the most modern boat in the fleet. Her design was 40 years old and certainly had never been envisaged for a circumnavigation. Newer boats, designed for the task, had failed along the way.

By modern standards *Suhaili* may have seemed over-spec. More to the point, though, she did the job she set out to do, albeit at an average speed of just four knots, and survived all the Southern Ocean could fling at her for five months.

So much has happened in the intervening years. Now we can sail solo round the world in a third of the time, the boats are technical marvels. Electronics now available leave the sailor with much more time to concentrate on sailing.

There is no need to be isolated as I was once my radio broke down two months into the voyage; the silicon chip ensures that the sailor is in permanent contact with his base for advice or weather forecasts.

Food and clothing are so much better, too, and watermakers have obviated the need for large water tanks, all helping to create faster and faster times. If the sailors are not so close to their environment, that is an inevitable result of progress.

The boats 30 years ago were smaller and heavier. They were built to survive in the almost unknown environment (to yachtsmen, anyway) of the Southern Ocean, and caution was the keyword. They carried a greater weight in food and stores because voyages were longer.

There were no EPIRBs, so if we got into trouble we were on our own, which probably meant lost. That alone made one conscious of the need to preserve things and keep everything together for another day, even if this caution cost a few miles.

Media criticism was restricted to comments on our foolhardiness for taking on something that was clearly impossible. However, if we wished to risk our lives that was none of their business. It is only when you call for help from someone else that it becomes everyone's business.

While there has been rather too much publicity surrounding certain rescues in recent years, in the current solo round the world race, Around Alone, the most serious so far was one performed by a fellow competitor. That the boat was probably unsuited for the ultimate conditions in which it was being sailed should be the cause of some serious thought by the designers.

Others in this year's race have lost rigs and gone aground. They will be left to reflect on the lack of concentration or a few kilos of saved weight that put them out of the event.

The fraction of a knot of additional speed becomes meaningless when the mast breaks. The objective has not been achieved and the mission has failed.

ALL THINGS BEING EQUAL

From Florence Arthaud to Ellen MacArthur, women give the boys a run for their money in solo long-distance racing. The reason why is simple – it's a sport that's far more about brains than brawn.

In February 2002 Ellen MacArthur claimed a magnificent second place in the Vendée Globe solo round the world race. Later Emma Richards entered the Around Alone. Both events illustrate that no barrier prevents women from competing at the top level of single-handed long-distance racing. Unlike in other sports (or even the sailing Olympics), this sort of competition needs no separate event for each sex.

Evidence of this exception to the usual run of things in sport has been growing for a while. French yachtswoman Florence Arthaud was giving the men a run for their money more than 20 years ago and

Isabelle Autissier proved she could beat a very good field. Now their mantle has crossed the Channel and is draped over the shoulders of two young and very competitive British girls.

Why is it that single-handing seems to be a field in which the girls can perform on equal terms and do not have to ask favours of anybody? It seems the sea and boats equalise opportunities in single-handing. Anne Davidson crossed the Atlantic decades ago, Nicolette Milnes-Walker made the first full crossing of the Atlantic in 1970 and Clare Francis participated in the single-handed transatlantic race and skippered a Whitbread Round the World Race entry.

In the teams and in shorter mixed events, the girls have yet to make their mark at the front, although there are signs that this may change. Tracy Edwards and her *Maiden* team produced a competitive result in the 1990 Whitbread and although the 2001 Volvo Ocean Race did not have an all-girls' team in the leading pack, this may have been owing to a lack of opportunities and time on the water. No one who has met Dawn Riley, manager of the all-female *America True* campaign for the 2000 America's Cup, can underestimate her determination.

Perhaps the reason for this success is that long-distance solo sailing is more a matter of mind than muscle. True, the girls tend to be smaller so their workload (for their size) has to be greater; their boats are as large as the men's, the loads as big, so it takes them a bit longer to perform a task and they use more energy doing it.

But that is not the main criterion. While being able to set a spinnaker or gybe quickly might make all the difference in a race in the Solent or sprint across the Channel, knowing when to perform them makes a greater difference when you are racing across oceans. Keeping an eye on tactics, watching the wind and making changes as soon as they are necessary matters far more than saving a few seconds because you are stronger. Working out which route to take to ensure your boat has its favoured wind tomorrow and the day after, that doesn't require muscle.

Instead, competitive advantage comes from a knowledge of weather patterns and how they develop, an attention to detail and in ensuring all the alternatives are covered. This is hard, solid, mental work. It does not appeal to everyone and it has never been the prerequisite of any one sex.

Alone in your boat, in the middle of an ocean where no one is watching, it is all too easy to roll over in your sleeping bag and decide to leave a task for a while. Those people with determination will climb out and deal with the situation there and then. A few minutes saved in a tack disappear very quickly if the boat is not sailing at its best speed and heading in the right direction. This has nothing to do with size and strength and everything to do with mental attitude. Getting maximum boat speed is highly desirable, but it is useless if you are not getting it in the right direction.

Our girls have been doing rather well in sailing: Shirley Robertson's Gold medal in Sydney, the first by a British woman in sailing, could be joined by others in Athens; Tracy and Ellen are due to attack the Jules Verne Trophy for the fastest boat round the world next year; and Emma is the sole British entry in Around Alone.

Better still, the media has taken these ladies to its heart and that attention means they find it easier to secure the sponsorship necessary to fulfil their ambitions. In this type of sailing at least, there is now equal opportunity.

NEVER TOO OLD
TO GO SOLO

When Japanese sailor Minoru Saito tied up in Tokyo Bay having overcome a legion of setbacks, he not only set a record for the oldest solo non-stop circumnavigator, he became a role model for us all.

A 71-year-old Japanese sailor called Minoru Saito arrived in Tokyo Bay in 2005 to become the oldest person to sail unassisted solo non-stop round the world. Minoru did not sail in the mould of modern record-breakers like Ellen MacArthur, but in the fashion of 40 years ago.

He set himself a target of 180 days, but took 234. During his passage – from Seabornia, south of Yokohama, down into the Pacific, around Cape Horn, past the Cape of Good Hope and then around Australia, before turning north for home – his average speed was only about five knots.

His 50ft boat *Shuten-Dohj II* – Drunkard's Child, irreverently chris-tened 'Shoot your doggy' by fellow round the world sailors – is not new, but an old friend Minoru has owned for 13 years. He enjoys being alone at sea with the wind and waves, but is no freak who sails on the ocean to avoid human company. Instead, while he likes his solitude, he is congenial company in port.

Short in stature and cheery, he has that total lack of pretension or arrogance which is often found in long-distance single-handers. They all know they have faced and survived the worst the seas can throw at them – this time, at least – so there is no need to try to talk up their voyages with those who have shared the same experience.

The sea is a great humbler. Somewhere out there will be conditions that could destroy you and the fact that you have survived is a source of gratitude not an opportunity to boast.

This is not Saito-san's first circumnavigation. He completed the 1990 BOC Challenge and the 1994 and 1998 Around Alone races, now rebranded as the Velux 5 Oceans, but he had never sailed non-stop round the world before. And this voyage proved a particularly tough challenge for the former heart patient. His generator failed completely, his engine gave up early on in the voyage, half his batteries failed and he had to rely on a couple of solar panels for all his electrical requirements. Many sailors would have given up with just one of those difficulties.

Communications inevitably became scarce through lack of battery power. On the positive side, however, this also meant he did not have a sponsor worrying him for messages, so he could choose to talk to the outside world when he had enough power and when he felt like it.

He experienced the almost inevitable knockdowns that the huge waves of the Southern Ocean inflict. Worse, his food almost ran out. Attempts to grow cress did not prove very successful – I tried with as little success mainly because I decided my drinking water, gathered from rain in the mainsail, was more important for me than the cress – and for the last month he lived on a diet of rice, noodles and a few vegetables. Healthy but lacking variety. But he never felt he was threatened and asked no one for assistance.

Four solo circumnavigations is impressive and if you take Minoru's voyages to and from the start of races, it adds up to a total of seven circumnavigations so far.[1] But most importantly, while most people retire at the age of 65, Minoru shows that the number of years you have survived is no measure of physical age and fitness.

Forty years ago Francis Chichester and Alex Rose completed circumnavigations at the official retirement age and their achievements were properly admired. Since then we seem to have developed a greater longevity and are staying fitter and more active long after we pass the official retirement age.

This increased age span and ability to use the time opens up a new world of opportunities. Unlike previous generations, we can aspire to a retirement when all those goals we dreamt about become possible. For sailors this can realistically mean setting out on that cruise round the world or perhaps continuing to race.

Agility may have declined (as I discovered recently when I raced a Laser for a day and spent the next two suffering with stiff legs) but the years of experience are an invaluable asset and it is a crime not to use it.

So, thanks a bunch, Minoru. You have set all of us a challenge. And just when I was thinking of how to plan my garden.

---

[1] Note: He has now done eight!

NETTED!

When a fishing line is caught around the keel of his Open 60 *Saga Insurance* while sailing alone in the Southern Ocean during the 2006 Velux 5 Oceans round the world race, Robin, then 61, was faced with a dilemma. Should he get into the cold, cold water and try to remove it?

I did not mean to heave to in a gale in the Southern Ocean. In fact, heaving to is a misnomer as I was anchored, very firmly, to a fishing net. *Saga Insurance* had been sailing along very nicely, thank you, averaging more than 12 knots and surfing up to 20 knots from time to time. Then suddenly the speed dropped.

I had been waiting for a front to pass with a big windshift and I thought this must be it, so I jumped up on deck. No, the wind was the same, but two lines were streaming out astern. I was surprised. I would not have expected two of my lines to have such a breaking effect. Then I realised they were not my lines.

At first I was incredulous. We might run into this sort of thing off the west coast of Ireland, but nets left lying around in the middle of the Southern Ocean? However, you cannot argue with a line around your keel and that is what I had.

The problem with these Open 60s is that they have a bulb keel so you cannot just persuade a rope to slip off; it gets firmly held in place above the bulb, which is 4.5m below the surface of the sea, so not easy to get at. There are a number of ways of dealing with this, none of which is going to be easy in 25 knots and 10m seas. The most obvious is to put a knife on the end of a pole and try to cut the rope. That's not as easy as it sounds. For a pole that long I only had batten material and nothing that length, so two shorter lengths had to be lashed together.

The boat is moving, even though anchored, and the pole gets moved about. Then you have to try to apply pressure when your arms are a foot apart and the lever is 15ft long. In effect, it is just not possible and I doubt it could be done easily even in the calm of a swimming pool.

The next method is to try to capture the line and bring it up to the deck or within reach of the deck so it can be cut. First you have to have a hook and it needs to be a strong one as the weights are considerable. Probably the best answer would be a grapnel. I thought about the kedge anchor but was worried it would get smashed into or through the side of the boat. My alternative hooks failed, just straightening out when the real weight came on.

I then tried pushing a float attached to a line – in this case an empty galley propane container – down on the end of the pole and then releasing it below the fishing line so it came up on the other side, effectively giving me a line round the anchor line. This nearly worked a couple of times, but the float, having surfaced satisfactorily, bobbed away out of reach.

I was very reluctantly coming to the conclusion that I was going to have to go for a swim, but by this time it was getting dark. There was nothing more I could do until I had daylight again.

As soon as the sky began to brighten the next morning, I prepared for the job. My concern was the very low seawater temperatures and the effect of the sudden shock on the body and its debilitating effect. With cold like that you lose strength quickly and I would have to haul myself back on board after some heavy physical work. The last time

I had done this in the Southern Ocean was on board *Condor* in the 1977 Whitbread Round the World Race when we got a sheet caught around the propeller after going back to pick up one of the crew who had fallen overside. That time I had a wetsuit, but very quickly lost all feeling in my feet, hands and face and had to be helped back on board. If that happened this time, without crew to assist me, I might very well not get back at all.

There was one change since the previous evening, one of the lines had parted and I could see its end floating about 40m away. It had not run through and cleared, however, because it had wrapped itself around the other part.

I put on a sailing drysuit, then a harness, attached it to a nice long line and went over the transom. I swam out as far as my safety line but could not get down to the main anchor line. I nearly reached it once, I think, but the boat surged and my safety line snatched me away. I lay there for a minute thinking.

Interesting watching the boat from maybe 100ft away. She was rolling horribly. I was also not too excited about the sudden attention of three albatross who clearly saw my floundering as some indication of a potential dinner in an hour or two. However, I could not stay here for long as I was becoming cold.

If I could not get hold of that main line we were stuck until something broke – and it might not be the line. The swing keel was taking all the weight and loadings and I was very aware of what had happened to another competitor, Alex Thomson's keel a week before [Thomson's *Hugo Boss* suffered severe keel failure in the Southern Ocean and he had to abandon ship in a dramatic rescue by Mike Golding]. I had to get that line cut somehow. One possibility was to swim further away from the boat to where it came closer to the surface, but before I did that I thought I'd see what I could do with the other bit of line.

I swam back to the boat with it. My hands were blue and losing feeling, but they worked well enough for me to haul myself back up and over the transom. Back aboard I winched in the line and, because it was twisted round the main line, it brought that close to the surface. Using an empty cooking propane container as a float, I attached a line to it, and then pushed it down with a batten to the uptide side of the line and then let go. It floated nicely up the other side of the line.

Now it was just down to brute force, hauling in on my messenger until the main anchor line was at the surface, at which point I was able to reach down and cut it with a hacksaw. We were free, but we still had a sizeable length of line caught around the keel – and if I sailed off with that there it could get caught around the rudders.

I then spent 20 minutes slowly removing the turns between the two lines with the aid of a batten, pushing the free end uptide as it were and letting it unfurl on the other side. Eventually the turns came out and the line could be pulled clear of the keel.

Freedom. But the price of the incident was the loss of a day's sailing and a position in the race. I wonder how many others have been caught on these free-floating lines left casually in the ocean. If we can all take the trouble not to throw plastic into the ocean I think fishermen could take the trouble not to abandon gear where it can become a hazard.

Because a hazard this certainly was. I doubt the boat could have taken another gale stuck like that.

MAD ADVENTURE

In June 2008 it was 40 years since Robin had set off on his voyage to become the first non-stop solo circumnavigator. He reminds us that, at the time, it was not even known if such a thing was possible and many believed that he would probably go mad . . .

1 4 June 2008 is a special anniversary for me as it marks exactly 40 years since I left Falmouth as a contestant in *The Sunday Times* Golden Globe race to try to become the first person ever to circumnavigate the world single-handed non-stop. This seemed to be the last big voyage left for yachtsmen at the time – although, of course, there have been plenty of other 'last big voyages' claiming that title since.

But the fact that this was how the voyage was perceived at the time provided added excitement and incentive. No one even knew whether such a voyage was possible. Francis Chichester had sailed round the world with one stop, but his boat had needed a big refit at the halfway point, so it was far from certain that a yacht could stay at sea for up to 10 months, totally self-sufficient and unassisted.

Nor could anyone tell whether a lone voyage of this duration would drive a sailor crazy. Indeed, many said it was not possible. I thought it might be possible and I had two big advantages over nearly all the other entrants. I was a Master Mariner, a professional seaman, and I had seen my boat built in India and subsequently sailed her home, which gave me an intimate knowledge of her behaviour in most conditions.

If I had any apprehension, it concerned the Southern Ocean and the huge waves that can be created there, something I had never seen in 14 years at sea, although I had been round the Cape of Good Hope a number of times. *Suhaili* was not a long, light thoroughbred that might outrun the waves, but a 10-ton double-ended 32-footer. However, her heaviness was due to her scantlings, so she was – and is – incredibly strong and robust.

In the 1960s sponsorship was in its infancy and wasn't really approved of in sailing circles. I wrote to more than 50 companies asking for support, but received negatives from all of them. In the end my only source of financial support came from writing as I went along.

The others received varying degrees of assistance, but my chances were blown when *The Sunday Times* reported that I did not stand a chance. In fact, the only journalist who gave me any credit was Bernard Hayman, Editor of *Yachting World*, but he had been in the Merchant Navy and knew how well we were trained and appreciated that I had a good few miles with my boat under my belt.

Someone asked how I was going to manage the problems of being alone and I answered quite honestly that I had no idea, but if I was back within two weeks I would not be coping with loneliness. In the end it was not a problem and I seldom felt bothered by it; there was just too much to do.

Originally, *The Sunday Times* planned to start their race in October 1968, but those of us with small boats were thinking about Cape Horn and the time it would take us to get there. We wanted to round the Cape in the southern mid-summer and with our lower speeds we had to sail earlier to achieve that. So they came up with two prizes, the

Golden Globe trophy for the first to complete the voyage and the sum of £5,000 for whoever made the fastest circumnavigation within their race.

I was the third to sail on 14 June 1968, after John Ridgway on 1 June and Chay Blyth on 8 June. Others followed at varying intervals. On 22 August the Frenchmen Bernard Moitessier and Loïck Fougeron set off and two days later retired British submarine commander Bill King. By this time both Ridgway and Blyth had retired. Nigel Tetley departed on 16 September in a trimaran. Italian Alex Carozzo and Briton Donald Crowhurst both left it to the last minute, sailing on 31 October. Carozzo pulled out two weeks later with stomach problems.

King and Fougeron had also retired by this point so the fleet was reduced to four: myself, Moitessier, Tetley and Crowhurst. None of us knew that Crowhurst was falsifying his reports and was never to leave the Atlantic – that news came some time after I had finished – so he always appeared to be a threat.

The voyage was not without mishaps. *Suhaili* started taking in rather a lot of water, about 200 gallons a day, through a working gap along her garboard before I reached the Equator. This was fixed by tacking a copper tingle along the seam on the outside – a long process because I could only put in one copper tack each breath as the seam was 5ft below sea level. I also lost the engine, not a problem as far as motion was concerned, but a valuable source of battery charging.

The Southern Ocean had proved how dangerous it was by mid-September. Early that month I was knocked down, losing all my fresh water and creating a leak in the deck which eventually shorted out the radio. I also had to dive into the freezing ocean and repair the self-steering. A really bad storm almost smashed *Suhaili* until I learnt that putting out warps from the stern swung her round stern to the waves and then she rode very comfortably in 30m waves.

The loss of water was made up by collecting rain in the mainsail. The loss of the radio did not worry me particularly. It was a huge effort to charge the batteries and try to get through with just 75 watts of power once a week but there were no alternatives. Satellite communications did not exist, which also meant there was no instant weather reporting as there is today, something that has greatly speeded times for circum-navigations as you can now tactically choose where to place your boat on the basis of reliable forecasts. Nor, of course, was there GPS or any safety back-up like EPIRBs or satphones.

But since we knew nothing of these future inventions we did not miss them. Once you lost communications then you were 'lost' to the world until you sighted a ship and they bothered to report you. I did get a report through via the Melbourne Pilot Vessel in early November and then again from New Zealand off Dunedin and that was the last anyone heard of me for four and a half months.

In the meantime, although lost to the world, I continued towards Cape Horn. Off New Zealand I learnt that Moitessier had been closing quickly to start with, but had slowed; Tetley was way behind and so, according to his accounts, was Crowhurst. And that was the last news I received until almost home.

I rounded Cape Horn on 17 January. It would have been earlier, but I had lost my self-steering off Australia and so was doing a lot of hand steering. Bernard Moitessier followed me 20 days later, having gained just over a week since New Zealand, although neither of us knew this at the time. He then decided not to finish and headed on around the world again to Tahiti. It is unlikely he would have caught me before I finished, but had he continued he would have won the prize for the fastest circumnavigation.

This left just Crowhurst and Tetley, as far as we knew. Tetley even-tually rounded Cape Horn in third place, but pushing to keep ahead of Crowhurst's claimed position, his boat broke up off the Azores. He came within 1,000 miles of completing the circumnavigation in what can best be described as a cruising trimaran, a significant voyage in anyone's terms, but particularly so in those days.

After passing the Falklands I ran into the South Atlantic high pressure system where I had one dismal day when I covered only nine miles. It was so calm I could not even hear ripples lapping against the hull. But this was followed by a glorious reach in the trades to the Equator. Calms again, with three days spent doubled up in pain with what later was identified as appendicitis, and then the long boring beat through the north-east trades.

Off the Azores I managed to get a message to the *Mobil Acme,* who duly reported my position to Lloyd's. Then picking up the westerlies, I headed back into Falmouth. It was only during that last week that I learnt about the rest of the fleet and discovered that I was going to be first back to my starting port.

JOY OF THE SOLO SAILOR

Only 173 people have sailed solo round the world, a small fraction of those who have climbed Everest. What is it that attracts them? Robin believes there is a purity in being alone with the elements, without outside interference or interruption.

The cult of single-handed sailing has come a long way in the 50 years since the OSTAR was first run in 1960. Then a race across the Atlantic was considered extreme and it had been difficult to find a yacht club to support the concept. Eventually, the late Col Jack Odling-Smee, commodore of the Royal Western Yacht Club of England took it on and the club continues to run it every four years, much to its credit.

There had been solo voyages before 1960, of course, but this was the first race. It attracted only five entrants, but the media loved it and a new sport was born. By the end of the decade there had been two more

OSTARs and confidence in the ability of yachts and sailors to make long solo voyages had grown and led to the ultimate sailing challenge, a non-stop round the world race.

Since those early days solo sailing has expanded enormously. Another transatlantic race has been introduced, the Route du Rhum, the BOC Challenge round the world was first run in 1982 and now we have the Velux 5 Oceans and the Vendée Globe, which first ran in 1989. Other short-handed events, such as the Figaro, have developed as a nursery for professional sailors wishing to establish a reputation. And for those who just want to enjoy the sport, the AZAB (Azores and back), solo or one-way two-handed, has been running successfully for a number of years.

All this has created heroes and heroines, and if the sheer number of events has diluted media interest, solo sailing can still be considered the ultimate in our sport. Only 173 people have sailed solo round the world, half of them non-stop, a small fraction (about 3%) of the number of people that have reached the summit of Mount Everest, which puts the extent of the challenge into perspective.

Where is the appeal of single-handed sailing? The main attraction, in my opinion, is the sheer pleasure of being alone at sea. There is a purity in being alone with the elements, without any outside influence, interference or interruption, working with the sea's rules.

I enjoy sailing with a crew, but the joy of solo sailing is the satisfaction of being reliant on yourself. If something goes wrong, there is no one else to blame or awaken to help you. Your decisions and mistakes affect you alone. There is also the pleasure of running your own life to your own rhythm, something increasingly rare on our overcrowded land mass.

But, as with everything else, the right to go solo sailing carries responsibilities as well. Respect for other users of the oceans is the primary one; avoiding asking others to put their lives at risk to rescue you if things go wrong. It is incumbent on every sailor to keep out of the way of other shipping and in a small yacht your vulnerability to larger commercial traffic makes this plain common sense.

To be a good and safe single-hander needs a high degree of self-reliance. It also requires a rather special degree of seamanship as a solo sailor has to be able to do everything on a boat themselves. For those sailing the oceans for pleasure there is no requirement to communicate, but the modern racer needs to keep their sponsors and the media informed, which conflicts with the essence of the sport, which is to be alone and untroubled by the outside world.

This was the hardest part for me when I completed the Velux 5 Oceans two years ago. I was out at sea, in the middle of an ocean, enjoying the solitude, and the satellite phone would ring. The intrusion into my reverie annoyed me, my instinctive reaction was to shout: "Leave me alone, I am happy out here just sailing and don't want to be bothered! Just send me an e-mail and I will look at it at a time that suits me, not a time that suits you, which may be when I am catching up on sleep or doing something on deck."

Those who need constant communication with the shore, beyond what is basically necessary, are not really natural single-handers, in my view, but the sport has become the thing that most professional sailors have to do to establish their reputations, so they suffer the loss of human contact to do it – to a degree, at least.

PART THREE

Safety at Sea

STEERING SENSE

Would most yachtsmen know what to do if they suddenly lost the rudder? Robin discusses different ways of effecting emergency steering.

E mergency steering is such a fundamental item of seamanship that perhaps it is taken for granted. Nine out of ten sailors can tell you what they would do in the case of losing or seriously damaging the rudder, but if the entrants in the 1995 ARC were typical, few will have attempted to put it into practice.

We are not talking about shipping the emergency tiller if the connections between the wheel and tiller break: this is about the rudder itself ceasing to function, a slightly greater risk these days with separate keels and rudders, and rudders without skegs.

Since it is not a difficult thing to practice, I was surprised that more ARC entrants had not amused their crews for an afternoon by locking the helm amidships and seeing what alternatives they could devise. (Locking the helm offset to one side is on the advanced course!)

Initially most would attempt to hold a desired course by balancing the sails. It takes much fiddling with the sheets and there will be frequent luffs into the wind before this is picked up, but worth the effort. It is quick and easy to do and involves no modifications or damage to the boat or fittings.

Such experiments can tell a crew a great deal about the balance of their boat and its general handling characteristics so it is never time wasted. A ketch or yawl is likely to prove easier to balance; hardening the mizzen will bring the boat's head to wind and vice versa.

It is worth reflecting that Chinese junks are steered almost entirely by use of the mizzen, the rudder acting as a trim tab-cum-daggerboard. If this system fails, or proves a bit too cranky, then the spinnaker pole over the stern is often recommended, with or without some sort of buckboard as a blade.

Experiments with a pole on its own from the stern of a Whitbread 60 as part of the round the world race committee's scrutiny (incidentally, this is the only race I know that asks the contestants to show how their emergency steering will work) proved this to be less positive than we'd anticipated.

Warps streamed on their own from each quarter, warps led from each quarter to some object trailed astern, the boat being steered by hauling in on the side you wish to turn have all been tried.

My personal preference is a large oar that can be held by a strop at the stern. The idea is as old as the rudder itself – indeed, this appears on Egyptian drawings dating back to 3000BC. They remained in common use up to the fourteenth century when the hinged hanging rudder became popular.

Merchant ships' lifeboats always carried one special oar, slightly longer than the others, for this purpose and it was a part of lifeboat drills to use it. The problem these days is finding such oars; the main market has disappeared with the decline of the merchant fleet, but nothing else is quite so robust.

Incidentally, such oars explain how starboard got its name. Steering oars were traditionally passed out over the right-hand side of the stern-post. The Vikings called the steering side of the vessel *styrbord*, which we easily corrupted into starboard.

Bord is a common suffix and appears in a number of European languages with variations on the prefix. In French, starboard is *tribord*, in German *steurboard*, Dutch *stuarbord*, Spanish *estribord*, all showing common derivation.

Port is an exception used in English, but this only officially replaced larboard in 1844 to avoid confusion. It is *bagbord* in Danish, *barbord* in French and Spanish, *bakbord* in German and Dutch. There is no definitive reason for the steering oar being shipped on the starboard side, but the word larboard might be a clue. It may be a corruption for ladebord, from the loading port which was usually on the port side so vessels would have to come portside to a wharf or jetty. If this were the case, it would make sense to have the steering oar on the opposite side to protect it and keep it out of the way.

So, when using a steering oar, tradition says launch it over the starboard side, but if anyone knows another reason for this perhaps they would write and tell me?

A STERN LESSON

The prevention of broaching in heavy weather has exercised seamen's minds since man first went offshore. Over centuries, they worked out with native wit what has now been scientifically confirmed.

A drogue or sea anchor is recommended in Special Regulations Category 0 for monohulls and Category 1 for multihulls in order to prevent a boat from slewing before a wave and broaching.

But drogues, cones or parachutes are not necessarily the ideal answer; they produce a heavy loading on themselves and the boat as they grip, are expensive to buy and have no other purpose. All seagoing yachts should be able to prevent themselves broaching, but why choose the most expensive, complicated and not necessarily the best solution?

Left to itself, a boat, surfing down a wave, will broach round in front of the oncoming wave and be rolled. Up to a point this accident can be avoided by steering to counter the swing, but as speed increases, the rudder tends to bite less well and sometimes full helm will not correct the course.

A steering oar is better: anyone who has watched a surfboat being guided in to a beach will have observed the increased turning force which can be applied, but even this is not always sufficient.

Something dragged astern of the boat not only acts as a brake, it also provides some directional stability. The drag prevents the boat from slewing.

Experiments by the Wolfson Institute in Southampton have confirmed that a boat, when end on to the sea, is repeatedly prevented from slewing sideways and being rolled – scientific support of what was learnt by seamen from experience over the centuries, in my case the hard way nearly 30 years ago when frightened in a Southern Ocean storm.

I could have streamed a sea anchor – if I'd had one on board – but I didn't because previous use in a ship's lifeboat had shown that the drag comes on immediately, which can be dangerous to the hands, and the painter can easily become tangled with the tripping line, making recovery difficult.

When you need to stream a sea anchor the boat is moving quite quickly before the seas, and the deck of a small yacht in a storm is not a good place to lay everything out, neat and tidy, prior to streaming.

Once streamed, the anchor grips effectively in the water and is pretty immovable. This means that the whole weight of the boat will be thrown on the painter or its holding point.

Try putting a line onto a pontoon, leaving 100ft of slack, and then motoring hard away until the line becomes taut. You will get some idea of the sort of strain that will be generated out at sea when lying to a sea anchor.

The cheapest, simplest and kindest solution to the problem is a simple warp. Streamed in sufficient length in a bight from either side of the stern, rope provides a considerable drag.

The total length should be about 20 times the boat's length and both ends should be secured to something firm and strong, such as the sheet winches. The advantages over a drogue are that it is much easier to stream under control, the amount of warp can be adjusted and when a heavy strain comes on a warp there is some give, so the winches or other hard points are not given such a sudden shock load.

The final factor is that warp has other uses and can be augmented with the anchor or kedge anchor warps, thus using something that already exists aboard and not causing unnecessary additional expense. Tied together with a diamond carrick bend, they are not going to come loose and this is a breaking knot, like a bowline, and can be undone easily.

They worked for aboard *Suhaili* in hurricane force winds, and were pretty effective with our multihull *ENZA* although we could have done with more line.

SMALL STEPS TO
DISASTER

No accident is the result of a single cause, an official report said in 1999, and it's true that it's generally a chain of small errors and mis-judgments, combined with sheer bad luck, that leads to disaster.

The Marine Accident Investigation Branch (MAIB) published a *Safety Digest* in 1999 analysing a number of incidents which led to, or narrowly avoided, the loss of vessels or lives. The report does not try to apportion blame or determine liability, but is written in a clear, factual manner to advise mariners and emphasise the lessons to be learnt. The step by step accounts of circumstances that led up to an accident and the conclusions drawn make sober and fascinating reading.

As the report states: "No accident is the result of a single cause" and it goes on to show how one simple lapse can start a chain of events that might ultimately lead to tragedy.

The loss of the sail-training ship *Maria Assumpta* in 1995 off Cornwall is one example of how just one minor decision could lead to disaster. The skipper decided to ignore the recommended route set out in the *Admiralty Sailing Directions* for approaching Padstow and take the inshore route between Newland and Pentire Point because he had used it before. If nothing else had gone wrong, this would have worked well and the vessel would have arrived safely.

The brig was close-hauled, with little room to manoeuvre, but she had two good engines, which had already been run that day without problems and the skipper felt comfortable that they could back him up if necessary.

When it became obvious that he was not going to clear The Mouls, he started the engines, his fallback, but now he had nothing else to fall back upon. Under power and sail he cleared The Mouls, but then both engines stopped.

There was little sea room to manoeuvre under sail. Wearing was too dangerous, with cliffs under the lee and tacking considered impossible on account of the sea and swell, so there was no choice but to try to press on and sail clear of the next headland. The skipper had run out of options. The ship struck Rumps Point.

Lifejackets had not been issued as they were stowed below. The report is critical of this, stating: "A skipper is ultimately responsible for the safety of his ship and all on board. Although every effort must be made to avoid a potential disaster, part of the skipper's mind must think through what needs to be done in the event of things going wrong."

While we can all say that there but for the grace of God go I, we should also remind ourselves of the lesson here: we must think things through in any given situation and imagine what we would do if the fallback plan fails. The MAIB conclusions make clear that a skipper should always have this in mind.

Another case covers the loss of four young men in the Sound of Iona. They were motoring home, on a dark night, across the sound in a 4.3m dinghy, having attended a ceilidh, when the bow nosed into a wave taking on a great deal of water. Although they immediately started to bale, the gunwale then dipped and the dinghy capsized.

One of the crew reached shore and raised the alarm. The others, last heard talking as they held onto the dinghy, were never seen alive again. None was wearing a lifejacket.

There is a timely paragraph, which hits close to home: "There is growing evidence to indicate that the most experienced yachtsmen are often the most reluctant to wear [lifejackets]. Even the oldest, boldest and most weather-beaten sailor can get it wrong sometimes. Always wear a lifejacket. Apart from anything else, it sets the right example."

SAFETY BEHIND CLOSED DOORS

How much faith should we put in the illusory safety of a liferaft? They are fragile and are easily punctured or torn. Better by far to make the yacht itself as safe as it could possibly be, believes Robin.

S urvival rafts are seen as the ultimate refuge. If the boat is in danger of sinking we take to them in the strong and fervent hope that this small capsule will protect us until rescue arrives.

But how much confidence should we put in them? Sailors who took to their survival rafts in the 1998 Sydney to Hobart Race did not all fare well. Some lives were lost because a raft tore to pieces – they are pretty fragile, not nearly as robust as a yacht, and are easily punctured or torn.

Of course, they work beautifully during training in a swimming pool, but the situation is vastly different in a storm at sea and they have been known to break up or capsize and drown their occupants. Swimming pool exercises familiarise people with the raft, but they can lead to a false sense of security.

Sailors must carry a back-up craft and we have yet to invent anything better than the survival raft as a means of allowing crew to abandon ship – few yachts can carry a lifeboat – so until there is a better solution, survival rafts are the only answer.

But we should look carefully at our boats to prevent our ever needing to use the raft. If you think about it, it is a risk to take to sea in an open, undivided yacht that has a large weight hanging beneath it fighting to haul it down. As soon as the yacht is holed, water pours in to help the keel sink the boat.

However, if the boat were subdivided, the leak could be restricted to a fraction of the hull volume while the rest of the space provides buoyancy and a dry living shelter for the crew while the problem is tackled. Subdivisions can also isolate a fire and starve it of oxygen.

So how many yachts have watertight subdivisions? Multihulls do, despite the fact that they have no keel. The organisers of multihull racing realised the dangers of capsize early on (they were more prevalent then than they are today) and decreed that all racing multis must have watertight bulkheads and an escape hatch that could be exited if the boat was upside-down. As a result, even if they do capsize, multis won't sink, so the crew can remain aboard, where they have shelter and are a more visible target for searchers.

Certain monohull classes also insist on watertight subdivision. This was first introduced by the Open 60 class in the 1980s and has been extended to the Open 50s and 40s. And any yacht operating commercially, such as in charter work or races like the Clipper Round the World Race, also has to have watertight bulkheads after the Maritime and Coastguard Agency introduced it as a requirement. But you rarely see them in the average private yacht.

Originally, small open boats were used near the coast. When they went further afield they were provided with decks. Where decks were not possible, as in ship's lifeboats, buoyancy was provided so that a boat would not sink even if it filled. Larger vessels had bulkheads since they were designed for longer oceanic voyages. Many dinghy classes have built-in buoyancy although they seldom stray far from land and do not carry a heavy keel. Perhaps it is time we reflected on what experience taught our predecessors.

Perhaps the real reason for the lack of watertight bulkheads is they are inconvenient when a boat's interior is being designed. To work effectively they must be spread throughout the structure so no single compartment, when flooded, will sink the boat.

Subdivision restricts the open spaces that are such an attractive feature of modern boats. It also requires strong watertight doors capable of withholding a full head of water from either side – so say goodbye to those beautiful teak doors.

Incorporating them would mean a radical change in yacht interior design, but at some point we have to address the question of what a yacht is designed for. If it is to be taken to sea, then it makes sense to make it as safe as possible to survive in this dangerous environment. So walk around the autumn boat shows and see how many of the yachts designed for ocean passages on sale have watertight subdivision.

THE TROUBLES OF 'IVAN THE TERRIBLE'

Californian Ivan Rusch dubbed himself 'Ivan the Terrible' and lifeboat crews in the English Channel in 2003 doubtless agreed after sailing to his aid six times in as many weeks. But the true cause of his failure was his abuse of the freedom of the seas, says Robin.

I van Rusch, self-described as 'Ivan the Terrible', made the headlines in May 2003. In a very short space of time, lifeboats were sent to help this 78-year-old Californian, who is single-handing from Belgium to the Mediterranean, on six occasions: off the Belgian coast, when he was in a shipping lane with an engine that would not start; when he was aground off Hastings, which he had mistaken for East-bourne; when the Portsmouth lifeboat escorted him into its port; when he was grounded in Poole Harbour and had to be towed off; when he was escorted into Brixham; and in difficulties off Start Point, when a fisherman jumped aboard and assisted in taking the boat to Salcombe then helped him sail to Plymouth, which is where I met him.

My first impression was of a pleasant, active man living in a mess. The deck was cluttered with a dinghy, solar panels and lashings for bits and pieces everywhere. Below was even worse.

This might be OK in the relatively benign conditions off California, but where strong and changeable winds are frequent a boat's stores must be well stowed and her decks uncluttered to avoid tangles if fast manoeuvring is required. Put simply, the boat was not shipshape.

Although Ivan was 78 years old, age was not the problem – plenty of people sail beyond these years and I certainly hope to. But I also hope I will adjust to my reduced agility and physical stamina and plan my voyages so they are within my and the boat's capabilities. And those plans have to include anticipating things not going to plan!

Ivan sailed with crew from California to Sweden via the English Channel. His problems began when he tried to sail single-handed. The Channel is no place for single-handing for more than a daysail and as a result starting and finishing ports within a suitable distance must be found. There is so much traffic here that to over- or under-shoot and risk staying at sea is asking for trouble.

But Ivan's problem was not just an ill-thought passage plan. He also had no charts of the ports he intended to visit so was disorientated by port and harbour lights. Nor had he thought about alternative havens and bought their charts. He complained about the cost of charts so when unsure of his location, he called the Coastguard and was surprised when a lifeboat appeared.

Of course a lifeboat appeared. If the Coastguard thinks someone is in difficulties, it will call for the lifeboat to deal with the problem before it becomes a disaster. A single chart costs £12, to launch an all-weather lifeboat costs close to £6,000. Half a dozen charts of ports along the English south coast would have saved close to £30,000 in unnecessary lifeboat launches.

Ivan Rusch may have crossed the Atlantic, but there is a huge difference between sailing in empty space and being restricted by land and busy shipping. The Channel can be dangerous, but provided you fully check the weather and ensure the chosen destination is within reach in the expected conditions, and have worked out the tides and have a chart of the destination, plus thought about alternatives, it need not be.

Americans love the word freedom. So do I, but it is not just a word to be chanted, it is a concept to be followed. The freedom to go to sea and be master of your destiny means accepting responsibility for yourself, your crew and your boat, assisting others if necessary, but managing your boat so you do not require assistance.

It means being properly prepared, with the right equipment and a clear passage plan. You cannot claim the right to freedom if exercising it costs others in inconvenience or by putting their lives at risk. Lifeboat volunteers frequently risk their lives to assist others and they should not be considered just another service like the AA.

To call out lifeboats six times in as many weeks indicates a stubborn refusal to accept personal limitations and that is poor seamanship. We might all require the services of a lifeboat at some time, but it is nothing to boast about.

ENERGY TO SURVIVE

Did you know that a 50p dextrose drink could be the most important item in your grab-bag? Robin learns why there is a high risk of dying in the first three hours after taking to a liferaft

Survival at sea is something that many of us may take for granted. We sign up and do the course, learn quite a lot, but how many of us think disaster is ever going to befall us? Even if it does, well, most of us sail close to the coast and rescue will only be a short time away, won't it?

Not necessarily. If you have not managed to get off a distress signal, rescue may be quite a long time coming and dependent on a chance sighting, which means you might have to survive in the water or on a liferaft for some considerable time. Cold will kill you eventually and in northern European waters that won't take all that long, even in the warmer seas of late summer. And other killers can finish you off before the cold.

One element of the survival and medical courses that we undertook in preparation for the Velux 5 Oceans in 2006 was an interesting talk by John Leach on the psychology of survival. One point that struck all of us was the statistically high risk of dying within the first three hours in the event of taking to a liferaft.

We all know that a liferaft is a last resort – they are small, not easy for rescuers to see and are vulnerable to whatever the elements throw at them. An EPIRB and SART deployed from the raft will make a huge difference and Velux regulations state that we must have one in our grab-bag. But how many cruising yachts do the same?

Liferafts can turn over easily, especially if the drogue is not deployed and this may involve climbing into a freezing sea and pulling it upright again, with all the loss of energy that involves. Even if you are wearing a survival suit, which would prevent you from suffering from hypothermia, how many times could you pull your liferaft upright before you tire, or miss a handhold and drift away from the raft?

All the research shows that you are far better off staying in your boat if you possibly can – and short of collision or fire, you are likely to be able to stay in it, especially if it has watertight bulkheads which separate the hull into independent compartments. Liferafts are there to be stepped up into, not down.

Yet supposing you have taken to the liferaft, why are you so vulnerable and why is it that 95% of those who die in liferafts do so within those first three hours? The answer is interesting.

During the exertion and psychological strain involved in dealing with whatever emergency occurred, you have been under stress and using adrenalin in large quantities. This means you have burnt a lot of sugar; indeed, you may have burnt up so much that your body has drawn on the sugar reserves stored in organs such as the liver. And if you have not eaten recently, no other new supplies are available. So your reserves of sugar have been seriously depleted or gone.

You are also likely to be dehydrated, so your blood volume is low and the blood pressure drops. Your naturally occurring hormones, such as cortisone, become depleted. You may not realise it, but your body is not in a good way at all.

Once in the liferaft, you may finally feel safe and relax, perhaps you could even drop off to sleep as you are bound to be tired. You may not wake up. Your body is probably far weaker than you appreciate and the sugar needs to be replaced – and quickly – or else you will go into shutdown mode. The answer is to take dextrose as soon as you enter the liferaft to replace lost sugar and start the body's recovery. Ideally, take it in liquid form because then you are also tackling dehydration.

After the talk, all of us who were preparing to set off around the world immediately added dextrose to the shopping list for our grab-bags. Even if you are staying in the boat after dealing with an emergency that has disabled it, dextrose or any high-energy sugar drink is a sensible thing to take once everything has settled down.

There is also a psychological element to survival, and those who instinctively fight for their lives are much more likely to live. This will to live is likely to be weakened if you are tired, so requires a greater effort at a time when you may least feel like making it. But if you want to live, you must make that effort.

ONE HAND FOR THE SHIP

Narrow decks, steep ladders, ropes and boom flying, heeling over – it's hardly surprising that accidents happen aboard yachts. But if you've safety-proofed the boat and taught new crew how to move about on board, you can really help to reduce the risk, says Robin.

Accidents to boats from collisions, grounding, fire, hull damage and the like always attract attention. As well as noting any drama that may make the news, most of us will read up a rather more carefully prepared account to see what lessons might be learnt. Personal accidents such as someone falling overside, or being injured by a boom might make the news, especially if they are fatal or require evacuation, but how many accidents take place on yachts that never warrant this attention, but cause injury to crew members?

Look at a yacht; the potential for accidents is high. Boats tend to have narrow access between deck and cabin with steep, small-stepped ladders, sometimes varnished and without a gripping tread. On deck, booms and ropes are flying around when tacking or if the boat goes onto her side in a squall. A person losing their grip when a large wave strikes or the boat pounds heavily is in a potentially dangerous situation because they could stumble across a heeling cabin or deck, resulting in a jar at best, bruises or even a broken limb.

In commercial shipping, slips, trips and falls are the most common cause of injuries and I suspect the same applies on yachts. We can deal with some of the common causes, many of which will occur when a boat has just been delivered. Sharp corners on furniture or deckhouses are like hungry rocks, awaiting the arrival of the unwary. Isolated bolts on deck await the unshod toe.

We can put covers on bolts, cut solid rubber balls in half, hollow out the centre to make space for the bolt head and use sealant to secure them to the deck over bolts and on top of any exposed bolts down below. I was once flung across the cabin of a large boat. I put out my hand to check myself and punctured my palm when it hit an exposed bolt.

Elsewhere, we can put anti-skid material on steps and we can work our way around a boat checking whether we have sufficient hand-holds in the right places. Look for the distance it is possible to fall if the boat goes over. The larger the boat and wider the cabin, the greater the potential for injury. A glistening gelcoated deck may look lovely in the marina, but be a serious slip risk once wet and heeled at sea.

A crew being rushed or pressured to do a job quickly, as happens when racing, can be particularly vulnerable. No one wants to be the person who slowed down a manoeuvre, so attention is on getting the job done, not on what would be normal safety procedures. Training can reduce these risks by making the job so familiar it becomes automatic, complete with the safety aspects, thus speeding up the actual performance of the evolution which removes the pressure to hurry. A small mistake in carrying out a task is likely to lose far more time than is lost by someone taking their time to do it safely.

In the end, though, it all comes down to experience and briefing of new crew. I have always thought it self-defeating to take new crew out in anything above a Force 4 because they are going to wonder – quite reasonably – what on earth is happening to them and how safe they are and probably lose their enthusiasm.

Even small things such as tearing their new oilskins on an uncovered bolt is discouraging. Allow them to get used to the unfamiliar sensation of their 'home' heeling over and understand movement is going to be slower because it is not so easy to move about. They must not feel they have to stand in the wind, trying to balance on unsteady legs because that is what Gregory Peck did in some film. Remind them to keep their centre of gravity low and not to be afraid of crawling around if they feel insecure.

The most important thing is to build confidence in this new and unfamiliar world. The old sailing ship adage of one hand for yourself and one for the ship is just as applicable on a small yacht as it was on the topmast yard of a square rigger rounding Cape Horn.

MAN OVERBOARD

One second the crewman had unclipped to go below, the next he had slipped into the sea. An incident in the 2009 Clipper Round the World Race reminds Robin that, however experienced the sailor, everyone can learn from a man-overboard situation.

N o matter how many times we may write about it, every man-overboard incident presents us with an opportunity to learn something new.

In November 2009 some 1,000 miles from Cape Town in the South Atlantic during the Clipper Round the World Race, 51-year-old Arthur Bowers went overboard from the yacht *Hull & Humber*.

Quite by chance we have film of him going overside. The camera was following an albatross behind the helmsman and just happened to aim at Bowers as he was unclipping his harness at the companionway before heading below. The boat gave a lurch as it went over a wave and he lost his balance and slid overboard.

It is the speed with which he disappeared that is so shocking. He tumbled straight from the cockpit and slid across the deck and under the guardrails in a matter of seconds – how often would you normally snag on the guardrails? It took 17 minutes to get him back.

But not everyone is so lucky. In a more recent case the boat managed to return to the casualty, but was unable to get hold of them and they either drowned or had a heart attack.

Before dealing with some of the problems of recovery, there are lessons that can be applied to prevent crew going over. First, always keep your weight low on deck, so that if you tumble you don't fall so hard, accelerate or topple over the guardrails. Sit down if there is no reason to stand.

Second, you may think you are well balanced and feeling the roll and pitch of the boat, but waves are not always predictable and this can throw you off balance. The third lesson is not to undo the tether on your harness until you are in the hatchway in rough conditions. The unexpected roll that sent Bowers overside came just as he was standing by the hatch and had already undone his tether prior to going below.

The fourth lesson is: always practise your MOB drill and make sure all new crew members are aware of the procedures. If nothing else, this will draw their attention to the risk and remind them not to fall overboard in the first place.

Recovery is always a problem and the greater the freeboard the more difficult it is. I am a strong believer in coming back to weather of the casualty as once the boat stops alongside it will tend to drift away to leeward. The casualty seldom seems threatened if they are alongside amidships. If they cannot be reached from the deck – and their hands are numb or they are in shock so they cannot help themselves up a boarding ladder – another crewman is going to have to go into the water and attach a line to them.

Ideally, this person should be on the end of a halyard, so they can be winched back aboard easily. They take down another halyard to attach to the safety harness of the casualty. If the latter is not wearing a harness, a strop needs to be put around them, but one that tightens as little as possible around the chest.

In our experience, a helicopter strop was very difficult to get around someone in the water on account of its buoyancy. In ideal circumstances the casualty should be hauled aboard in the horizontal position, but this will cause delays and time may not be on your side.

As always, the most vital point is not to lose sight of the man overboard. The well-tried system of one or two crew members doing nothing but point at the person in the water, and the more modern MOB button on the GPS/plotter are both essential, but keeping sight at night can be difficult.

We are all required to carry danbuoys attached to liferings with a light and dye marker. The issue is that this can become entangled very easily, so deploying it becomes a nightmare – a problem 30 years ago that remains today because nothing has been done in the meantime.

Perhaps those who insist that we carry this kit (and doubtless mean well) should go to sea and try to deploy it. Then we can hope to have something that is practical to use rather than something that seems to tick boxes for a person navigating a desk. We need a way to find someone who has fallen over, but we need something that is easy to deploy and reliable.

PART FOUR

Life on Board

REFLECTIONS ON
A RECORD

In 1994 Robin completed his second record circumnavigation, this time with a co-skipper, Peter Blake, and a full crew. And though he found the food monotonous, the company occasionally irksome and the labour hard, there were compensations – not least going round in 74 days instead of 312!

Seventy-four days at sea with hard labour, without sighting land and cooped up with the same seven companions may not seem the perfect way of life, particularly when the food lacks chewability – but the compensation was that *ENZA New Zealand*'s was not a longer voyage.

Compared with the voyage in *Suhaili* 25 years before, the speed was four times as fast and there was the advantage of a fit young crew to share the workload. Against this was the lack of variety in our food: our own fault, especially once the frying pan was lost over the side, which removed the possibility of any pretence of a fry-up.

During a long time at sea, meals assume great importance since they provide variety each day. Otherwise days merge into each other.

While the company meant having somebody to talk to, I occasionally found it an irritation when, lost in my private thoughts just looking at the sea, someone asked a question or made a statement that required an answer.

On balance, having companions was better than not, although towards the end we had just about exhausted every topic of conversation.

The actual distance is more impressive in some respects than the time. In miles it was the equivalent of 45 Fastnet Races, but only 37 if the record were to be broken each time. The highlights were probably icebergs, huge tabular bergs the size of St James's Park and taller than Nelson's Column; the pod of six killer whales that pursued us for a mile or two at 17 knots before they decided that we didn't look interesting enough to eat; and the storm just before Cape Horn.

Each provided excitement, although the storm, while intellectually fascinating in the matter of ship-handling through waves in excess of 60ft, was not something anyone would rush to repeat.

It is not always realised that ocean racing is as much a question of meteorology as clever sail trimming. There is little point in having expert trimmers if the boat is not sailing the shortest distance, and in ocean racing the quickest route is not necessarily geographically the shortest.

This was the first time I had experienced the benefits of having a router advising where the boat should be placed to gain most from the changing weather patterns. It is unquestionably an advantage. Not only can routers access far more information, but they can sit quietly and analyse it without the interruptions that are part of life aboard.

It is fair to say that our man's advice led to our gaining the 1,500 mile lead we obtained as we passed through the South Atlantic High, whereas our rival Olivier de Kersauson's router failed to guide him round the centre and he was almost becalmed for three days. Although this lead was reduced to 400 miles later by adverse weather, it was a cushion we were able to hang onto right to the finish.

Our beating de Kersauson's trimaran does nothing to prove that a catamaran is superior to a trimaran. The difference between the two boats lay in the philosophy adopted by the skippers. We believed in paying a small weight penalty for the advantage of additional crew as a reserve against injury and to avoid becoming over-tired.

We always had three men on deck, whereas de Kerasauson often had only one, so we could sail harder, knowing that even if one person was off deck, as was the case for nearly two weeks, it would not affect our performance. Being less tired also meant that our thinking was fresher.

Our record time of under 75 days will be hard to beat by an existing craft because we had about average luck – more or less favourable for the first half of the voyage and equally unfavourable for the second. Although we had 28 days when our day's run exceeded 400 miles, we had nine where this was less than 200. Our worst was 88 miles.

Sooner or later our time will be beaten, of course, but the boat that does it will probably be nearer 120ft long than 100ft. While I dream about that, I am going to take a short holiday aboard something larger (if less speedy) and navigate the *Sir Winston Churchill* in this summer's Tall Ships Race.

But as Ratty in *The Wind in the Willows* would have agreed, I am sure, it's not the *kind* of boat – it's just having one to mess about in that matters. . .

NIGHT TERRORS

Gybing, changing sail or taking in a reef is often a tricky operation at sea, but in the dark it is doubly dangerous. Robin sheds some light on the subject of night sailing.

I t's nighttime. A second reef is being put in and the reefing line has to be cleared. The boom end is within reach of anyone standing on the deck, but as most of us do, the crewman leans against it to steady himself as the boat rolls.

Suddenly, for no apparent reason, the mainsheet comes free and the crewman, caught off balance, topples overside. He is not clipped on and not wearing a lifejacket. Although the boat is turned quickly, the casualty cannot be found. It's one of those accidents that no one could have anticipated, leading to a tragic waste of life.

Why should the mainsheet suddenly slacken? It's in a good make of jammer, but it must have come unlocked or perhaps was accidentally unlocked by someone. The trouble was it was dark and no one saw the danger.

A scenario such as this can happen all too easily. Once, while I was stowing *Suhaili*'s mainsail in a storm off Cape Finisterre, she rolled and I went swinging outboard, hanging onto the main boom. The crew went to the lifebuoy, to be checked by my frantic yell to harden the mainsheet, which should have been tight.

I did not have a safety harness on, but I was wearing a lifejacket. None of us knew why the sheet was slack, but at least that story had a happier ending.

We sometimes forget what large and powerful machines yachts are and what heavy equipment has to be controlled to sail them. Considerable forces are exerted to move a few tons at eight or more knots – think of the horsepower utilised by an engine to do the same thing – and these forces focus into the strain on the rig and tension on the halyards, sheets and guys.

Just because they do not make the noise of an internal combustion engine does not mean that the forces are not in action – their silence makes them easy to ignore. But when they break or are let go, we are rudely reminded of the potential danger of the equipment with which we are working.

The running rigging may be simple enough to understand and operate during daylight hours, but the situation can be far more dangerous at night.

I have had novice crew who, in daylight, were unable to put their hands instinctively on the mainsheet and runners even after 10 days at sea, so imagine the chaos they could cause if they tried to operate anything in the cockpit in the dark. (They were 'allowed to leave' since they were clearly a danger to their shipmates.)

We all try to keep lights out of the cockpit in order to avoid ruining the night vision of the crew on deck, but people, particularly new or inexperienced crew, can easily make a mistake in these circumstances and, for instance, let off the spinnaker pole topping lift rather than the guy when tripping that sail, thereby threatening injury to the foredeck hand.

A torch can help, of course, but the degree to which it helps depends upon the power, and if it is powerful and shines into someone's eyes, they are dazzled for a while and thereby rendered useless.

I think we had the right solution to this aboard *ENZA New Zealand* when we sailed round the world in 1993. It was our policy to switch the deck floodlights on the spreaders whenever we had the crew on deck for an evaluation such as a gybe or sail change. (When tacking or reefing, the gear was simpler and so this was not always necessary.)

Fishing boats, oil rigs and other working vessels have always used floodlights on their decks at sea when necessary and there is no reason why yachts should not do the same. Once these lights are on, it is possible for everyone on deck to see what they are doing. Better still, they can see what others are up to, and tasks are carried out quicker and more safely as a result.

The helmsman and lookout lose their full night vision, of course, but you can have a good check around the horizon before lights come on to see if there is anything to keep an eye on and they can be switched off the moment the evaluation is complete.

The lights give warning to other vessels of the yacht's existence – assuming they are keeping a lookout, of course. And the temporary loss of night vision is a small price to pay for adding to the crew's safety.

PROSE FOR POSTERITY –
A LOG FOR LIFE

A logbook should not be looked on merely as a means of recording your noon position and cataloguing sail changes; it is a record of your entire sailing history, says Robin.

At the end of the season I go through my logbooks and make an analysis of the season's sailing. Then I add them to the long shelf at home full of logbooks. They date from 1965, when *Suhaili* sailed from Bombay, and extend right through to last weekend's cruise.

They cover boats as diverse as a 92ft catamaran (the Jules Verne circumnavigation in the multihull *ENZA New Zealand*) and the Sail Training Association's topsail schooner *Malcolm Miller*, and every one of the over half a million miles I have sailed – with the exception of one race from La Rochelle to Gulfport, Mississippi, when the French charterers walked off with the book, even though it was written in English!

In that row of books is encapsulated my sailing life. The logbook is an essential part of the navigation equipment of a boat. In it should go all fixes, bearings, position lines, GPS fixes, course, error of the compass, speed, wind, barometer and weather conditions – everything you might wish to refer to later.

A good log should allow anyone to calculate where the vessel was every few hours, thus enabling the boat that loses all power from its navigation instruments to be able to work out an accurate dead reckoning and get safely to its destination.

The Merchant Navy trained me to keep a log properly. They had to be accurate and no errors were allowed. If a mistake was made, it had to be crossed out and initialled, so that it would be clear at any enquiry that a change had been made.

But just because the log might be produced as evidence in the event of an accident does not mean that it cannot be written for general interest as well. Sightings of anything of interest should go in, such as ships and marine life, sail changes, anything the crew are doing aboard the boat – it helps to recapture the flavour of a particular voyage.

My entries showed a noticeable change when our daughter was about 12 years old and to encourage her enthusiasm we took to selecting postcards of ports and anchorages visited and pasting them into the logbook where gaps allowed. If we visited a port more than once, the card had to be different, and then a competition developed to find the oldest or most amusing one.

There is another note from that era referring to a blue-hulled 'ferry' with three cream masts sighted at anchor off the island of Rhum!

Such entries bring back happy memories and at the back, on a spare page, I have kept a record of the crew who sailed with me along with their addresses, many out of date, some only dimly remembered.

Some years ago, when I was researching a rather interesting case of an East Indiaman abandoned in the 1730s, I went to the East India Library in London and asked to see the logbook. After 10 minutes it was produced – a large, leather-bound book filled with copperplate writing, but the entries were as clear and understandable as a ship's log of today.

The incident I wanted – the abandonment of the Captain and officers, but not some of the seamen – appeared in less than three lines, but there it was, documented.

When we were organising the first BOC Challenge, we decided to give a valuable prize of a sextant to the writer of the best log from among the competitors. This was not just altruism: we hoped it would give us some valuable quotes.

The winner wrote a fascinating log, a very clear and interesting account of his circumnavigation which must be a treasure to him now. The runner-up was good, and then there was a gap. The bulk of them were so-so, and the poorest came from one of the most experienced sailors in the fleet who confined himself to entering the date and the noon position only.

This was doubly sad as he had picked up one of his fellow competitors who had had to abandon his boat, and has no record of the incident. We had more information on how the situation had developed at race headquarters, but we could never have the full picture.

The Indiaman's little-known adventure can be read 260 years later; the BOC rescue will probably be forgotten – just because the log was not kept.

WIDE OPEN SPACES

The larger the boat and the more palatial the accommodation, the harder it is to live aboard in heavy weather – but there are compensations. . .

I t was the whale's fault. I was asleep when the commotion on deck woke me, caused by a 30ft whale jumping about 30 metres off the starboard side. Of course, by the time I had appreciated what was going on, got myself up and gone to the porthole of my cabin to take a look, there were not even any signs of disturbed water.

There was an hour left before I was due on watch, an awkward amount as even if I did manage to drop off to sleep, I would be woken almost immediately. So I lay back and thought of the gale that was forecast.

It was expected to close with us from the west by late evening or perhaps early the following morning, passing – according to the weather centre at Washington – some 120 miles north of our track. If the proximity was a little fine, at least the winds would be westerly, but they would bring a rising sea. Up to 12ft had been predicted and that would be uncomfortable even in an 86-footer.

We were competing in the Atlantic Challenge and, like most of the other competitors, were not aboard a racing boat, but a very comfortable cruiser designed for the waters of the Caribbean or Mediterranean during their respective seasons. Our draught was a mere 8ft which meant we slipped sideways very effectively when on the wind, creating a frustrating drag, but leeway is with you when the winds are abaft the beam.

Our lack of a deep keel meant that we slid a bit and lacked the damping effect on the rolling motion which depth gives a boat. The main effect of three days of strong winds and rough seas (which would become more complicated and confused as the winds veered), meant that living aboard would become less easy.

Comfort is relative. To someone in a small boat a gale is extremely unpleasant and dangerous, but to a passenger on the *Oriana* it may not mean more than putting on a coat when venturing on deck.

In yachts, I suspect that size creates a false sense of security. Large yachts should ride larger seas more easily, but somehow it seems wrong that the more palatial surroundings are moving at all, let alone being subjected to the indignity of having wet oilskins draped in their highly polished chart houses.

In practice, the sheer space in a yacht designed for Caribbean cruising makes it somewhat difficult to live in at sea as there is a greater distance to fall in the cabins, and the designers and builders won't put in handholds that might ruin the décor.

The result is that you have to crawl on hands and knees across wide open spaces, whereas in a smaller boat you can probably put a hand out either side to the deckhouse for steadiness.

In the meantime, I was starting to slide down to the leeward side of my wide berth as we heeled more. The basics of simple living with three days battened down are to get your gear well stowed so that it won't move, regardless of which tack the boat is on or how much she is thrown about, and to try to keep as dry and comfortable as possible.

Life was different on an 80-footer somehow, and a higher standard of appearance seemed appropriate, so, in view of the time at my disposal and the impending reduction in habitability, I decided to indulge in the luxury of a warm shower.

In most yachts in transoceanic races where facilities have been limited, it has always been my policy to wash in seawater as early as possible as it is antiseptic and keeps the skin clean, not an unimportant matter when a lot of people, working hard physically, are forced to live in close proximity.

But in the past there had never been the option of a daily shower so there was no alternative. Perhaps the advent of efficient watermakers that convert seawater into fresh makes this a foretaste of things to come, but a boarding school and Navy background makes me look upon such luxuries with guilt and consider them thoroughly character deforming – and the gale never fully developed anyway!

ROUGH TREATMENT

A medical emergency far from land is one of a skipper's worst nightmares. Robin himself contracted appendicitis 10 days from land, so what did he do? He reached for the *Ship Captain's Medical Guide*.

There can be few greater fears for anyone at sea than having a medical problem halfway across an ocean when you're cut off from any immediate assistance. I find external injuries much easier to deal with than some mysterious internal pain. My imagination runs riot when I cannot identify the problem and I reach for the *Ship's Captain's Medical Guide* for guidance. This is set out for the non-medical man with a list of symptoms – very helpful. But even if you can identify the problem it may be too serious to be treated aboard.

Appendicitis springs to mind. What can you do when one of the crew contracts that and the boat is two weeks from land? This happened to me when sailing round the world alone without a functioning radio.

The *Ship's Captain's Medical Guide* was quite clear on my symptoms – I was either pregnant or had appendicitis. Its solution was to seek assistance, but the radio wasn't working and the nearest land was at least 10 days away. A passing ship ignored my flares and even a distress rocket as it sailed past a quarter of a mile away.

I went onto a soft diet: canned milk, porridge and milk-soaked biscuits. The pain, which was enough to prevent sleep, lasted for a couple of days and then disappeared and I put it down to poisoning myself with my own cooking. But 18 months later, when the problem reappeared, the surgeon told me there had been a lesion on the appendix he had just removed. I had been incredibly lucky.

Before setting out on a long voyage the crew's medical history should be checked to pinpoint any specialist requirements. It is also worth checking up on the symptoms that can indicate a past condition is recurring and learn what action to take. Most boats carry a full medical kit and qualified medical advice is at the end of a telephone or radio. The advantage of the latter system is that it puts you quickly in touch with proper medical advice and also alerts the safety centres, who can see if there is any appropriate assistance near to hand.

Before departure, it is worth checking the medical kit. The *Ship's Captain's Medical Guide* has a comprehensive list (perhaps too comprehensive) but the problem is what would you leave out? Bandages, disinfectant, burn ointment, pain killers and eye lotion may be all you've usually needed, but suppose there is a serious injury or illness and the lack of the right medicines threatens life? You would never forgive yourself. And what antibiotics should you take and what will they cure?

Drugs have a limited shelf-life and become less effective with age. Those containing morphine have to be stored somewhere that can be locked. Check all use-by dates to ensure anything beyond its life can be replaced during the voyage. Keep a separate notebook to log the use of any drugs that require a doctor's prescription. Some drugs need refrigerated storage. This presents no problem if the boat has a refrigerator, but there needs to be a fall-back plan in case of power failure.

There are some useful medical courses for professional seamen such as the Ship's Captain's Medical, but the RYA also runs a one-day first aid course. (Their one-day sea survival course is also worth doing. Indeed, both are essential for yachtsmen making long voyages.) However, the course only really equips crew to handle first aid and is not designed to deal with complex emergencies.

Even if there is a doctor aboard and however good the attention, it is doubtful anything can be done other than to stabilise a situation and a small, tossing boat is far from an ideal ward for a seriously ill or injured patient. The best course is to get the patient to proper attention ashore or to a passing vessel that can provide medical attention as speedily as possible.

A FINE BALANCE

Even if they're from the same mould, no two boats behave in the same way under sail, says Robin, and it's only by playing with trim, sail plan and even stowage that sailors can really get to know their boats.

Balancing a yacht is a black art. No two boats are the same and even boats from the same mould can show idiosyncratic differences.

Modern yachts tend to be a little bit unbalanced. This is because the stern of modern designs is often wider than the bow sections, so more area is immersed aft as the heel increases, which creates extra buoyancy there. The inevitable result is to change the trim as the stern lifts and this pushes the bow down.

Apart from increasing weather helm, a lower bow when pushing to windward tends to throw more water across the deck – fun on a day race, perhaps, but not attractive when cruising. In terms of structure, there is not much anyone can do about this; the problem is in-built. Adding ballast aft using a water tank or moving crew aft can provide some correction.

If the boat has weather helm close-hauled and appears to lie to the waterline as drawn by her naval architect when upright, the solution is to alter the balance between headsails and mainsail.

The ideal situation is to have slight weather helm with all plain sail set and no increase in the helm required when the wind rises. But if the helm is more than five degrees, then start adjusting the tension on the sheets. This will help to indicate where the problem lies.

Often a boat may not need much helm in light breezes, but requires a lot when the wind rises. This does not necessarily demand a change of sail plan – changing the rake of the mast often does the trick and is the first thing to try. Increase the rake aft by loosening off the forestay and tightening the backstay and then go out for a trial sail.

Some weather helm is an advantage – apart from building up arm muscles, it means that if anything happens to the helmsman the boat will fly up into the wind. However, whenever the rudder is moved from the centreline it starts to apply drag, so a sail imbalance that requires a lot of helm will mean slower progress.

Traditionally, it has always been thought that the lead (the distance between the centre of effort and the centre of lateral resistance) is all-important. It can be. A moment's thought will tell you, though, that the moment you change or reef a sail, the position of the centre of effort must change and, consequently, so should the feel on the helm. Sometimes it does, but with another design of boat it may not be perceptible.

The wind pressure on the sails and their shape and angle to the wind also make a difference to the boat's balance. When sailing close-hauled there is a greater heeling pressure and thus less effort going into forward motion, but as the boat pays off, she will come more upright and this will change the feel of the helm.

Some boats, with all plain sail set, will sail along close-hauled with the helm loose. Others require it to be lashed. Take down the mainsail and it is surprising how often a boat will come up a bit rather than paying off downwind as you might expect.

Two identical boats from the same mould should have broadly similar sailing qualities, but differences will be emphasised if loads are placed in different places. As an experiment, try moving your crew forward and then aft when close-hauled; the change in helm, speed and comfort can be remarkable.

The placing of stores and equipment or water and fuel will also affect performance – a factor few of us consider when stowing gear. Weight amidships can make a boat lively, which can bring on seasickness among the crew, and if it is spread along the length of the boat or stowed more at the ends, she may pitch heavily.

A naval architect may be the one who designs the boat, but it is up to the sailor to find out how to get the best from her. Never be afraid to experiment when sailing and never be put off if the experiment does not work. You will be learning more about your boat every time and that brings greater confidence and safety.

SEWING LESSONS

Nowhere is the adage a stitch in time saves nine more apt than on a yacht, where ignoring an unravelling sail seam can mean hours of work later. But how many yachtsmen know how to effect proper repairs? says Robin.

A while ago I was looking at the remains of the ensign from the *USS Chesapeake. HMS Shannon* captured this frigate after a furious 15-minute action off Boston in 1813. The ensign was being restored at the National Maritime Museum at Greenwich and the stitching caught my attention. The stripes, which are about all that remain of it, were carefully stitched using 'fore and aft' stitches, not sailor's stitches, so the flag had probably been made ashore by supporters.

Landsmen will tell you the expression 'a stitch in time saves nine' refers to repairs to shoes. If you talk to a sailor, it refers to sail repairs. How many of us have watched a couple of stitches part on a sail's seam and quickly dropped the sail for repair before the whole seam goes? Were shoes more important than sails to the ancients and which required more care? It's a point for debate, but the fact remains that my shoe might hold out for a few days after one stitch has gone, but my sail certainly will not.

Early sails were made from palm leaves and reeds. When the ability to spin and weave cotton was established, this material quickly became popular because it was more efficient and easier to handle. There is also a suspicion that some early sailors used wool, including the Vikings – imagine the weight of these sails when they got wet. Flax became the standard material eventually and although cotton continued to be used for yachts, flax canvas took over in the commercial world.

Now we have man-made fibres. Terylene/Dacron can still be stitched, but some of the latest materials do not respond well to the small holes stitching causes and a film material has no grip for twine so glue has replaced stitching. Nevertheless, stitching is still used on most yachts' sails.

But do people really know how to repair a sail properly?

The sailmaker's tools are simple. A sailmaker's needle, a palm with the indented 'iron', sailhook and thread. Chandlers sell yachtsmen's palms, which are rather light; a real palm is a much stronger and safer instrument.

The sailmaker's hook is to hold the material so the stitch can be tightened against something. It is stuck into the cloth at the beginning of the seam and its lanyard secured to something firm. The type of twine will depend on the thickness of the canvas. Needles come in a variety of sizes to suit different materials. They are triangular in shape and should be kept clean. If rust develops on their surface they will be harder to use and can damage the material.

Stitching a sail requires one side of the material to be laid over the other, overlapping by an inch. Flax canvas used to have a blue thread about an inch from the edge, called the selvedge stripe, which made a good line for the overlap. Most Dacron does not have this, but it can be drawn on with a pencil. Start by pushing the needle down through the material you are sewing to, then twist it so it comes back up through the material you are sewing on.

Use the selvedge line as a guide, insert on the inner side of the line and come back up on the other side closer to the edge of the canvas.

You are aiming to have the stitches evenly spaced at about four to an inch for normal work. Initially this will not be easy; it takes practice, but if there is a long seam to sew it pays to get the stitching neat early on as it will be stronger, not to mention look better.

If a lightweight material is being repaired, such as a tear in a spinnaker, use a herringbone stitch to hold the two sides of the tear together before putting sticky repair tape over the damage. Basically you make a round stitch to hold the two sides together, but bring the needle up behind the newest stitch and over it to make the next one. Don't over-tighten the stitch as it will distort the material. The idea is to provide some additional strength to the sail to assist the repair tape and the stitching should be just tight enough to allow the material to lie flat without any creases.

Never leave a sail set if a hole appears or a seam begins to part. It does not matter whether the old adage is for cobblers or sailmakers, if you leave a known tear to the wind you will have at least nine stitches to put in and probably a lot more.

PRESERVED IN SALT

Fresh water is bad news for wooden boats and rain-soaked timbers soon rot as micro-organisms flourish. Which is why a happy boat is one whose timbers are regularly pickled by a douse of saltwater.

Nothing is more depressing than opening a laid-up boat and getting a whiff of mould and long stagnant bilges. Damp has permeated everywhere and mould has spread, the boat feels dead and, indeed, it is dying. All the materials that created it have been untended all winter and now they are decaying as surely as if they had been thrown on a rubbish dump.

Part of the problem is that however hard one tries, salt gets below and the crystals attract moisture. Everything needs to be washed down to clear the salt away. Well, not quite everything if the boat is wooden or has wooden decks. Salt may be damaging to metal and soft materials, but it can be the kiss of life for timber.

Freshwater rots boat timber faster than anything else. We protect it with paint, but this does not stop all moisture – think how doors and windows in a house shrink in summer and jam in winter even though they are painted. Moisture is getting through however many coats of paint are applied and in time this moisture will cause rot because it allows micro-organisms to flourish.

To prevent this happening to a boat the timbers need to be 'pickled' with salt. It was not just because the mate or first lieutenant liked a clean deck that wooden decks were washed down every morning on ships. It was also to keep them salted and stop them drying out in hot climates.

Anyone who has seen a vessel laid up will notice how quickly rain darkens the timber. Then before too long moss appears and the timber starts to rot. It is a problem faced by ships tied alongside for long periods or put on display – they need salt.

The same applies to boats laid up in freshwater basins. After a while their planks will rot. It was estimated that the fleet of warships built on the Great Lakes of Canada during the war with the United States in 1812 could be expected to last no more than 10 years as they would always be in a freshwater environment.

Owners of wooden boats on rivers like the Thames can put the longevity of their timbers down to their boats being smaller than com-mercial craft like Thames barges and the fact that they can keep one side dry. Timber beams in a house can last for hundreds of years but expose them to the elements and they will rot within 10 years. One is always dry, the other is not.

Ideally wooden boats need to be exercised at sea from time to time just to allow saltwater to get back into the timbers. (This is not a bad idea anyway, as the weed that grows on the hull in saltwater usually dies when the boat is put in freshwater and vice versa.) Brixham fishermen used to drop salt licks into their bilges to keep the salt content high. Or look around old dockyards and you will discover a mast pond. Suitable mast and spar timber was dropped into it and left to pickle. This preserved the wood and avoided it getting shakes, those cracks that appear in most timbers if they are left to dry out.

Timber is organic and needs to be treated as a living material. If it cannot be given a regular soaking at sea then ensure it gets a good coat of a natural preservative such as linseed oil. It is not a bad idea to mix raw linseed oil with an equal quantity of wood preservative and apply that. This mix, being thinner, penetrates easier and the preservative will keep the timber free of bugs and rot.

We think of laying up a boat almost as resting it. The same applies to boats left alongside for the public to view or admire. Of course, there is more wear and tear on a craft that is in constant use, but it is also true that when a boat is used a lot all those little repair, maintenance and preservative tasks get done and the boat is lived in more.

The warmth from human habitation does not just make the boat feel better when you're in it, it is better for its whole structure. So next time you are leaving your boat for a prolonged period put in a greenhouse heater. It will keep everything dry and create a gentle circulation of the air inside the boat, which will help to preserve it.

READY OR KNOT?

Considering that knots are as much part of a seaman's tools of trade as a sharp knife or sturdy pliers, it's amazing how cavalier some sailors are when it comes to knowing the right hitch or bend for the job.

Why are some people so casual about tying knots? They either don't know the right knot to use or don't know how to tie it properly. Perhaps they feel that so long as the knot holds it does not matter which one it is, but a knot is rarely an end in itself. It is temporary and being able to untie it is as important as being able to tie it properly.

There are six basic knots everyone should know: reef knot, bowline, round turn and two half-hitches, the rolling hitch, clove hitch and sheet bend. I would add the carrick bend for reasons I will come to. Armed with these knots and knowing what each is for, a person becomes halfway to being useful about deck.

We use the term 'knot' to cover almost anything we do with a rope's end, but actually a knot is anything we do with an unravelled rope's end, like a splice. Tying two ropes together is a 'bend' and tying a rope to any object is a 'hitch'.

The bowline is probably one of the most useful and used knots. As Clipper crews know, I am liable to jump aboard and ask a crew to tie me a bowline. Failure to do so means I demonstrate again how it is done then sit with the crew until they have tied 10 correctly and consecutively. Fail on number nine and we start counting again at one. The repetition may be boring, but it is one way to help remember – tie a few each day for a while and you'll own the knot for life. So a little effort with the end of a sheet while waiting for a turn on the helm can bring dividends.

The main advantage of a bowline is that it is a breaking knot – it can be undone easily as the loop can be pushed over the standing part to loosen it. But crew need to be aware that it can come undone if it is not pulled tight before use, especially with slippery rope. A reef knot will break if the two ends are pushed towards each other.

If you are trying to tie two ropes of unequal size together a sheet bend is the right answer. If you lack confidence in your knot, the fallback is a bowline in the end of each rope. A clove hitch locks onto itself and is ideal for fenders and tying anything to a round bar or rope. It was used to secure ratlines on shrouds and the old sailors would not have used it unless they trusted it. A rolling hitch often comes in handy, but remember to put a couple of half hitches in before it if you are using it as the end of a stopper.

One of my favourites is the carrick bend. It is very easy to learn, like most good bends it looks right when made properly and it is also a breaking knot, with a loop at each end. Its main use is for joining together two ropes that are going to be under considerable tension, like hawsers or anchor cables.

I first saw it used in anger when we were trying to tie up a 7,500-ton ship in the Suez Canal. The mooring boat had been slow and a strong easterly wind was blowing us across the canal to the extent that we were almost at the end of the 8in sisal hawser. A spare was quickly tied to the end and the situation saved. Even Bertie, our mighty bosun, whose arms made Linford Christie's thighs look puny, couldn't break that one and we had to resort to a knife and resplice eyes in both ends. I have used a carrick bend ever since when putting out a bight astern in a storm or to extend the scope of the anchor cable and it has never let me down.

The trouble with breaking knots is that they are almost impossible to untie when under tension. Look around at other boats moored to a quay and see how many have used a bowline to make a loop. It's fine as it will hold but what happens if you need to slip the line in a hurry? The right knot for this is the round turn and two half-hitches as the half-hitches can be released if the rope is tight and there is still some restraint on the bollard or cleat because of the round turn.

Knots are as much a part of a seaman's tools of trade as a knife, spike or a pair of pliers. However, you cannot go into a chandlery and hand over a credit card to get them, you have to sit down and master them. The increased self-confidence is a more than adequate reward.

ANCHORS AWEIGH

As long as people have been going to sea in boats too cumbersome to haul up the beach, some form of anchor has been necessary – and anchoring is an art that all yachtsmen must master, says Robin.

We have been anchoring ever since someone decided he was tired of hauling his boat ashore, tied a bit of rope around a convenient stone and chucked it overside. It probably did not take long for people to realise the stone had to be carefully shaped so the rope did not slip off or better still have a hole in it, but two problems would have remained – stopping the stone from dragging along the bottom and chafe of the rope.

Dragging was a question of weight and grip. By Roman times the simple stone had developed into a fluke-like apparatus, with lead adding weight to help it dig in. However, this did not tackle the chafe problem as iron chain had yet to appear, so even if the anchor held, an outcrop of rock in the anchorage could quickly chafe through the cable as the boat swung.

Various solutions were tried – sewing leather around the lower end of the cable, as found on a fourteenth century wreck at Vejby, was one – but the problem was not solved until iron was cheap enough to forge into chain, which also applied a more horizontal pull and helped the anchor bite.

But before chain, early seafarers would soon have realised the advantages of mooring to reduce chafe and cut the risk of dragging as the weight came on the anchor from a new angle. By dropping one anchor upstream and another downstream, the boat could swing with each change of the tide, but the anchors remained put, which reduced the risk of snagging.

The boat brought up to its uptide anchor instead of swinging to a single one. The swinging circle, which would be twice the length of cable paid out for a single anchor, was much reduced as a result. In a narrow river this also helped prevent the boat swinging into a bank or drifting into other vessels in a busy anchorage.

The boat could be anchored by putting out one anchor over the bow and the other over the stern. But while this reduced the drift further, it meant the boat could not swing with the wind, which could place more strain on anchor cables, more of a problem before chain and man-made fibre ropes.

The anchor dropped, there was also a need to warn others where it had been laid to prevent fouling, so anchors came to be buoyed. The other advantage of buoying an anchor was that, should the cable part, the crew could find their anchor. It would have been quite common, too, to buoy the two anchors together if the boat was leaving the spot to go alongside and knew it would be coming back to the same place, especially in the days when anchors had to be weighed by hand.

A vessel either lies to her anchor or is moored when she uses more than one anchor. There are three basic types of mooring from a vessel. The ordinary or dropping moor requires the vessel to stem the tide, let go one anchor then drop back double the length of each scope of anchor cable required. Then let go the other anchor and haul in on the first one until the lengths are equal, or at a chosen unequal amount, bearing in mind the ebb usually flows more strongly than the flood.

A running moor is the reverse process. Round up into the tide and drop one anchor, then motor slowly upriver to double the length of cable required for both anchors and let go the other anchor. Then drop back heaving in on the cable of the first anchor until the desired amount of cable is out on each. The third method is to let go the main anchor then carry the kedge out in the dinghy, drop it and then tension the two cables.

If not moored fore and aft, it is essential to ensure that the boat swings the same way round with each tide to avoid the two anchor cables twisting around each other.

A swivel, joined to both cables, removes this problem, especially when the boat might remain moored for some time, but it is wise to leave the end of at least one cable or the shackle in a longer cable, near the hawsepipe or gammon, so it can be disconnected to remove twists if necessary.

And, of course, make sure that if you moor at high water, you will have sufficient water at low water to float within the swinging circle.

FOOD FOR THOUGHT

Far from living on hard tack and weevilly biscuit, sailors in Nelson's Navy were better fed
than yachtsmen today! Though Robin does rec-
ommend a good hotpot and plenty of pasta.

Those who think that hard tack and putrid meals, as served to the poor sailors who manned the warships in the Napoleonic Wars, are acceptable aboard yachts at sea these days, may have to rethink. I'm probably as guilty as any. Once out in an ocean I tend to live on stew – or pot mess as it would be called in the Navy – except that I'm a bit more selective about what goes into the pressure cooker. The Navy version, used on picket boats, was a large pot into which everything supplied by the Purser was tipped in at the start and just reheated as and when required.

There are advantages to this. The pressure cooker has a sealed lid which prevents the contents from spilling if the pot is overturned; the meal cooks more quickly; the contents tend to meld more speedily; and, provided the right selection of ingredients is used, it's hot, appetising and sustaining when eaten.

The reason for the rethink comes in a new book entitled *Feeding Nelson's Navy* by Janet Macdonald. Far from a diet of mouldy salt beef or pork, and biscuits that emitted weevils when tapped on a table, the evidence suggests that the sailors at the turn of the nineteenth century were remarkably well fed. Their weekly ration was generous, consisting of beef or salt beef or pork, 7lb of hard biscuit, pease, oatmeal, butter and cheese. When available, fresh provisions were supplied, including the all-important antiscorbutic fruits.

In all, it is estimated that the sailors' average daily intake amounted to 5,000 calories per day, considerably more than the daily recommendation of about 3,200 calories for a male today. Of course, these were men who were involved in heavy manual labour, not just in handling the sails but a gun weighing three tons. This required a huge physical effort from a crew of eight men to load, run out, swab and reload. The crews could hardly have maintained their average rate of fire, of close to twice that of the French, if they hadn't had the energy – and that came from their food.

In a prolonged action, too, it was the reserves of energy available that eventually paid off, and this came not only from the meal they'd just eaten, but the muscle power and stamina built up in months of hard training.

The Officers knew this, as did the Admiralty, which was why such a huge effort was made to supply plentiful and good quality ingredients wherever the ships were. The fleet train was not an American World War II invention; Nelson's fleet before Trafalgar had been at sea for a considerable period and was kept supplied by a sophisticated and efficient logistical tail.

Interestingly, when we were planning food for our Jules Verne Trophy attempt on *ENZA New Zealand* in 1993, the intake was planned at 6,000 calories per day. Even with all hands being called every time we did a sail change, and the fact that there were only eight to handle the sails – which would have called for 18 on a maxi yacht – this turned out to be more than was necessary.

I finished the voyage one stone heavier (7kg) and none of that was fat, but on being checked by the hospital, there was consternation when it was discovered that my cholesterol reading was 9.8 – five points above the recommended level. A crash diet involving stoppage of bacon, eggs and fried bread for breakfast, less meat and more fish brought this down eventually and to this day I can't see what all the fuss was about – I have seldom felt better!

Of course, most of the food on board was freeze-dried, but that does include things like pasta. So, although one got a bit tired of the menus after a couple of months, shortage of choice is inevitable when space, weight and high calorific content are required. On any voyage, the meals tend to be a high point in the day, so even rather mundane fare is more appreciated than it would be ashore.

So it appears that if we're going to feed ourselves in accordance with the Nelson tradition, we are going to have to buck up our ideas. The requirements? More imaginative menus, better selection and variety of ingredients, and a big enough helping to keep the crew filled with energy. They'll tack better for it!

KEEPING THE PEACE

It's a tough job being a skipper. Not only is he or she responsible for the boat and all the legal issues, but must deal efficiently with a diverse and not always harmonious crew. Robin has his own methods.

The dynamics of a crew at sea are a subject that has not been well explored. The key person is the skipper and it is a greater responsibility than most people appreciate. It includes the safe operation of the yacht as well as the safety of the crew and some legal liability if things go wrong. The sea is an alien environment and is often unpredictable and frightening. It can never be mastered completely, but experience does count.

Then there are all the rules that cover the interaction with other vessels, port rules as you depart and arrive, and how to call or respond in an emergency. There is also the vital issue of the provision of good meals, watchkeeping, and so on.

Into this strange pressure cooker we throw people, but not professional sailors, ordinary people whose normal job employs them five days a week and for whom sailing is a leisure pastime. They come in all types, backgrounds and levels of experience. Some are easy-going, some argumentative. Some are hard workers and some will skive. Some are fit, some not. Some pick up things quickly and with others you wonder if they can ever learn anything useful. Somehow such a polyglot mix has to be welded into an effective and happy crew and this is the skipper's job.

It is easier to keep a crew happy and motivated when the skipper is the most experienced member of the crew and also the owner, but sometimes this is not the case. Ownership is not necessarily such a strong support for authority when the boat is out at sea and people feel frightened. The worst scenario is where a crewmember is more experienced than the skipper and lets it be known. This will lead to challenges to authority, disruption as people take sides and confusion in a real emergency.

One of the most dangerous crewmembers will be the person who thinks they have learnt everything early on and starts to pontificate. This occasionally happens with Clipper Round the World Race crews and the answer is simple: move onto subjects that the person has not learnt, so they begin to appreciate that they are not as knowledgeable as they had thought and those they are trying to impress can see it. Experienced skippers have less of a problem as the wide and varied knowledge they have built up over the years will ensure they can always keep ahead.

The best method is to start by expecting all the crew to learn as the voyage progresses and showing them how much there is still to learn. The Almanac provides plenty of subjects that need to be mastered – just studying the collision regulations can keep people occupied for weeks!

But what happens if a conflict develops between two crewmembers? It so easily happens. Someone takes a dislike to the way another clears their throat, or leaves the gear lying around and the bickering starts. It takes time for people to learn to accept another's foibles, but there can be a lot of unrest until this happens. Soon the whole crew is suffering and it has to be stopped.

We had this on *Condor* in the Whitbread Round the World Race in 1977, when one crew from each watch took a dislike to each other.

Quiet talking achieved nothing so in desperation I decided to spend a day picking on them both. First I told the mate, Peter Blake, who was as frustrated as I was, so if my plan failed he could pick up the pieces!

Throughout the day, whenever the watch on deck made a mistake, I blamed the person who was having trouble with his fellow crewmember. I watched them respond with surprise, then anger and finally hatred of me. By evening, when we collected in the cockpit to go through the day and prepare for the night, they both chose to sit as far away from me as possible. But – they were talking to each other! They had found something in common, their dislike of me. The good news was that it broke their dislike of each other and, after a few days, they stopped disliking me too.

That was extreme, and I am sure is not taught by Human Resources or modern management courses, but we were 20 days from the next stop, nothing else had worked and I needed a crew to work together without hesitation.

PART FIVE

Ocean Rescue

TO GO OR NOT TO GO?

Whether or not to abandon ship is always a tough decision, but it rests with the skipper alone – no matter what pressure is brought to bear by others.

I n 1995 Isabelle Autissier was the latest in a long line of sailors to be faced with the horrible choice, when the boat is seriously damaged and help arrives, whether to struggle on and try to get the boat to shelter or to abandon and accept the offer of rescue.

The rescue vessel or helicopter may have come a considerable distance and at vast cost and it might seem ungrateful to say no to the offer. It is probably owned by a government with all the legal powers and PR effort that can mean to put pressure on a tired and shocked crew to give up.

This can start with the plain assumption that the sailor is going to abandon, then move to an order to do so, and even back it up with the threat that time is short, fuel is low, the rescuer cannot wait all day, will have to leave soon and may not be able to return if the situation deteriorates.

What might normally be seen as determination and courage on the part of a crew not to give up their ship are quickly perceived as stupidity by bureaucrats and media who have little idea of the sea or the true situation, and no conception of the feelings that build up between crew and boat.

In fact, Autissier had little choice. Her boat had a gash 5ft long in the deck, the aft compartment was flooded, the jury rig had gone and she was at 48°S, a long way from any port and experiencing stormy conditions. Furthermore, she was away from a regular shipping route so even if she did keep the boat afloat for a while, but needed to be picked up later, it was unlikely that other help would be at hand.

Tragically, too, her earlier dismasting meant she was at the back of the fleet, so the usual back-up of another competitor was not in existence, either. Clearly she needed support and a tow if she was to get her damaged boat to safety, so her life had to be the priority.

But it is not always so clear-cut. During the infamous 1979 Fastnet Race, some of the boats claimed that the helicopter crews told them that they could be rescued there and then, but if they didn't agree to being taken to safety at that moment, there was no guarantee that the helicopter would be able to return later.

Some of these crews, which included some very experienced offshore sailors, abandoned their craft as a result. A number of these were recovered later, still floating, even with their hatches wide open.

It is rather hard to apportion blame in the circumstances. The helicopter crews undoubtedly thought they were doing the right thing to save lives; the crew obviously felt the same; and anyone can be clever after the event.

I was faced with a somewhat similar situation in mid-Atlantic after being knocked down four times in a morning and eventually losing the masts. We were not in distress and continued under jury rig towards the Azores.

A US Navy aircraft found us and vectored a merchant ship to rescue us – an offer I refused, although the vessel ordered us to abandon, quoting the US Government as an authority. This refusal was not bravado: although she may not have looked it, *Suhaili* was perfectly sound, we were not in a gale, the crew were fit and supportive so we did not need rescuing.

Unfortunately, I had lost the radio and could not explain the situation. The rescuers meant well and no doubt thought they were doing the right thing, but they had absolutely no authority to order us to abandon. In yachts, as in merchant ships, the skipper takes responsibility for the safety of the boat and the lives of the crew.

The problem is that the average merchant ship has a professional crew who are likely to have a better understanding of the risks and what is at stake, whereas the experience of the crew aboard yachts varies considerably. When a professional tells them to abandon, it may seem foolhardy not to obey, but ultimately the final decision rests with the yacht's skipper and crew...

PRICE OF RESCUE

Yachting is, statistically, a rather safe sport – certainly safer than mountain climbing – yet a rescue at sea will always provoke an outcry about the cost.

Why is it that whenever there is a tragedy in a yacht race, the media become hysterical about the costs of the rescue effort? We saw it back in 1997 when Tony Bullimore was rescued during the single-handed Vendée Globe race and yet again during the 1998 Sydney-Hobart tragedy.

Every report seemed to demand to know why the race was not cancelled the moment the weather turned nasty and, more aggressively, why should an élite sport expect others to risk their lives rescuing foolhardy millionaires in their luxury yachts?

There was no such fuss when Richard Branson tried to balloon round the world, crashed into the sea and had to be rescued. Ballooning is hardly a sport open to everyone and yet it does not get put in the same category as yachting.

Similarly, there was no mention of the costs when three mountain rescue teams had to be deployed to attend an accident on Ben Nevis which eventually cost four lives.

In all three cases the relevant rescue services were on hand and mobilised to do what they are trained to do. But when this involves yachting, the media never fail to bring up the question of the cost.

Sport is physical and, by its very competitive nature, challenging. The harder the sport, the tougher the challenge and the more interesting it becomes. People will push to the limit and this can be dangerous.

But where is the interest if the objective is easy? Humans are programmed to rise to challenges. This is why we have developed to the top of the evolutionary tree. For many of us a life without real personal mental and physical challenges would be a life without colour or stimulus.

We react in differing ways to suit our characters, some climb mountains, some balloon round the world; those who feel the call of the sea search for the hardest races. A desire to accept challenges applies equally to those who join the rescue services.

Yachting is, statistically, a rather safe sport, certainly safer than mountaineering and, judging by recent balloon crashes, safer than that sport as well.

Those who took part in the Sydney-Hobart race accepted the danger that exists whenever a boat goes to sea, but they were not foolhardy. The fact that more than half the fleet withdrew from the race once they realised the extent of the approaching storm shows sensible seamanship. That some yachts were still overwhelmed, while seeking shelter, just shows the ferocity of the storm.

If the media pundits had their way, sailing in anything approaching a gale would be banned and the quality of seamanship among yachtsmen would inevitably fall. Sailing, like mountaineering, is a hands-on sport and competence can only be developed through experience.

The emergency services exist to save lives. Firemen are taken off their ordinary work each time they deploy to rescue a cat stuck up a tree, but they look upon it as a useful training exercise. Search and rescue teams are maintained by the Royal Air Force to recover pilots. Fortunately this does not happen often, but the teams keep their standards high with the other rescues they perform.

The same applies to Coastguard helicopter crews, lifeboat crews and the sailors on warships. The people who volunteer for the emergency services are the type of people who have chosen their profession because it provides a greater challenge in their own lives.

No one in their right mind courts danger, but accidents happen and so instead of bewailing the cost of the resulting rescue attempt, we should see them as opportunities to practise skills and gain the vital experience that maintains the high standards that exist.

DOCTOR ON CALL

When you have to transfer crew from one boat to another in mid-ocean, the accepted method by liferaft is not always the best, says Robin.

The accepted method of transferring someone from one boat to another at sea by means of a liferaft may not be the right answer in some conditions.

In the 1999 Clipper Round the World Race, one crewmember seriously injured his leg when the boat was careering downwind in gusts of up to 30 knots of wind and 15ft waves. A tourniquet was immediately applied to staunch the flow of blood, but it was obvious that, if the foot was to be saved, a person with medical experience was urgently needed aboard.

Fortunately, a competing yacht had a recently retired surgeon in its crew and was only 26 miles away. It responded immediately to the PAN-PAN call and arrived on the scene three hours later.

The seas were heavy so there was no question of the two yachts going alongside each other as this would have caused serious damage and probably injured more crew, so there were two alternative methods of effecting a transfer. One was to let the doctor swim across, wearing a lifejacket and harness with a safety line attached; the second was to use a liferaft.

The water was warm, about 25°C, but the decision was taken to go by the book, launch a liferaft with the doctor in it and then either tow this astern or throw a line so the other boat could come alongside and pick up the passenger.

The eight-person liferaft was launched with some difficulty and inflated. Unfortunately, it inflated upside-down and it took some time in the large seas to get it righted. The doctor boarded with difficulty and the painter was eased to allow the raft to float clear. At this point the raft's sea anchor brought up, but as the raft and yacht moved, this sea anchor caught around the skeg.

Trying to pull it clear broke the painter – they are meant to break under a certain strain, of course, so that when abandoning a yacht the liferaft does not get dragged down when the yacht sinks.

The doctor was now in the liferaft and in danger of being crushed as the stern rose and fell in the swell so he was brought back on board. Efforts to attach another line to the raft proved fruitless. This method was now abandoned.

The priority was to get the doctor to the patient, so the raft was left caught under the counter and a line thrown to the other boat, which came close in alongside for the purpose. This line was led to a block amidships on the receiving boat, where there was least danger of the doctor being crushed and freeboard was at its minimum. The line was attached to the doctor's harness and a retaining line secured just in case. The doctor then jumped into the sea and was hauled across the narrow gap and lifted aboard in less than half a minute.

The liferaft was proving extremely difficult to disentangle from the skeg. Now half full of water, the raft had no points to which to attach any line to heave it aboard and it was too heavy to be lifted by its canopy.

Since it could not be recovered nor left floating around in case it started a search and rescue alert, it was slashed to deflate it and the bits hauled back on board.

In this incident the liferaft proved to be a distraction. The doctor could have been transferred quite quickly, probably within 10 minutes if the lifejacket, harness and line method had been used from the start. Instead, almost an hour was wasted.

The view of those involved was that it would be better not to bother with the raft if this happened again and just use the line system. Even in cold water the doctor would be in the water for such a short time he would not have time to get really cold.

ESCAPE FROM THE PERFECT STORM

Forget what you saw in the Hollywood film, says Robin, the story of *The Perfect Storm*, as told by the US Coast Guard, is a tale of superb decision making and seamanship and holds lessons for us all.

The film *The Perfect Storm* attracted considerable interest in 2000 but it was Hollywood and the facts got lost in the need for good theatre. I was lucky enough to hear an account first-hand from the captain of the US Coast Guard cutter involved in the dramatic rescues.

The film's title is an oxymoron for a seaman. No storm is nice, let alone perfect, but the conditions did produce something that meteorologists might refer to in this manner. The captain of the cutter had a large number of very difficult decisions to make, most of which he got right, and that raises some interesting points.

First the rescue of the downed helicopter crew, when all but one crew were saved. The cutter was rolling 110° (forget the film, where it suddenly stabilised as the men were hauled from the water). A net was thrown overside just forward of the bridge for the casualties to grab. This position was chosen as it could be seen from the bridge and was away from the bow. Waves were reaching an estimated 80ft and the cutter, all 1,600 tons of it, was pitching to the extent that the rudders and propellers were frequently out of the water.

With the bow doing the same, approaching a casualty without crushing them was no mean feat. It was achieved by lying beam on to the seas, hence the huge rolls, and adjusting the ship to bring the casualties on the beam in line with the net. It was a superb piece of handling and had to be repeated a number of times. Once the casualties had grabbed the net, a team on deck, who were putting their own lives at risk just being there, hauled them up.

Why not use a rigid inflatable (RIB)? Well, it had already been smashed recovering the crew of a yacht and its crew had had to be recovered by helicopter. In any case, if the cutter went bow to the sea the RIB was swamped and if it tried to provide shelter by making a lee its rolling made the recovery extremely dangerous as the fall was slack one minute and cannoning the RIB against the ship's side the next. It might have been an option in a normal storm, but not this one.

The point for yachtsmen to note, however, is that when a liferaft was tried from the ditched helicopter it was blown away like tumbleweed in a Western. It was simply not an option. Helicopters do not like putting their winch wire anywhere near a mast. It's OK in the film, where it miraculously unwound, but in real life it would snag and that means the aircrew must cut the wire instantly or ditch themselves.

A helicopter without a winch wire is no longer a rescue helicopter. If the liferaft cannot be used to get the crew clear of this danger, then they are going to have to go into the water if they are to be picked up safely. Helicopter crews don't mind this – they train for it – but it is a bit of a shock for the crew as they have to leave the apparent safety of their boat, individually, to allow the air crew to get at them.

Why individually? Because usually only one person is picked up at a time and unless the crew have a survival suit on they are going to get extremely cold if they wait in the water. This is often the biggest problem – persuading a frightened and demoralised crew that they should leave the perceived safety of the boat one at a time and throw themselves into a raging sea.

An alternative is to ditch the mast and give the helicopter a safe run – after all, if you are abandoning ship the mast has no further use for you. But this can be dangerous in itself in these sorts of conditions. As you release the shrouds and stays the mast might fall in any direction, a threat to anyone else on deck, and once it has gone overside it can become a battering ram, smashing holes in the hull. This may not matter too much if you are about to be hauled away, but it can provide a deathtrap as dangerous as a spider's web to a fly if you have to go into the sea.

What is made quite clear by incidents like this, time and again, is that knowledge of how to behave and how rescue authorities act, hugely increases the chances of rescue. Investment in a sea survival course is money well spent.

PART SIX

The Southern Ocean

LIFE IN THE FAST LANE

The noise, the stinging rain, the biting cold, the exhaustion of a record-breaking run across the Southern Ocean in 1994 makes Robin wonder why he does it. And then he takes the helm. . .

The vibration is relentless. If it's not caused by a sail, then it's the hulls bouncing along the top of the waves as our catamaran *ENZA New Zealand* hurtles through the Southern Ocean, heading for Cape Horn.

Here in the nacelle in the centre of the boat the noise is less, but we get the smashes as a wave hits the underneath, lifting you from your bunk and jerking you rudely awake. Down in the hulls it's a constant roar, a cross between a tube train and being inside a car in an overenthusiastic carwash.

Life has revolved round steering, sleeping, sail changing and eating for four weeks now, as we crash eastwards, but it's the discomforts that dominate the daily pattern, particularly waking up after too little sleep to find and climb into clammy wet foulweather gear. Then it's out on deck for three more hours of stinging cold.

There are two types of rain, described by their effect on the skin, soft and hard. Then there is hail. That really hurts.

You wonder why you do it until you take the helm and control the immense power that *ENZA* generates. Then everything else is ignored as the mind concentrates on holding a steady, safe and fast course.

This is what we came for, the unbeatable, exhilarating sensation of running our easting down faster than it has ever been done before under sail. At the helm there is a continuous hiss from the water rushing past the sterns. It is so constant that you have to listen for it.

If you want a target, the GPS showing the changing longitude is sufficient. Hold your breath for a minute and watch the longitude change more than a third of a mile; try for two and when you take your next breath, seven or eight cables have run beneath the boat.

To put the speed into some sort of perspective, 25 years ago I averaged four knots for my circumnavigation in *Suhaili*, which took 312 days. In *ENZA* we are averaging more than four times that, but of course we need to, if we are to achieve our target of 77 days.

We calculated that it would take us 33 days to sail from level with Tristan da Cunha to Cape Horn. At the latitudes we have chosen, not too far south to avoid heavy seas which will slow us down, this means we must average 410 nautical miles in a day. That's 17 knots. So far we have done it, but then we have an incentive – once round the Cape we can turn left, it will get warmer and we shall be able to see a level horizon once more. Just 8,000 miles to the finish line and 25 days to do it in...[1]

---

[1] The above account was made while Robin, along with co-skipper Peter Blake and the crew of the 92ft catamaran *ENZA New Zealand*, were attempting to beat the round the world record for a vessel under sail, at that time 77 days set by *Commodore Explorer*. The current record, set in March 2010, is 48 days 7 hours and 45 minutes, held by the 103ft French trimaran *Groupama 3*.

CALL OF THE SOUTH

The Southern Ocean is as much of a challenge to seafarers as climbing the whole Himalayan range would be to a mountaineer. Huge waves, high winds, icebergs and freezing temperatures make it the ultimate in a yachtsman's experience.

The Southern Ocean is very special. It is for sailors what climbing Everest is for mountaineers, or perhaps more appropriately the equivalent of climbing the whole Himalayan range, as the ocean has no single peak. Neither area is now inaccessible, but both still offer the ultimate challenge in their respective sport.

The Southern Ocean extends 15,270 miles around the world at a mean latitude of 45°S and 13,900 miles at 50°S. Nowhere else does an ocean girdle the globe and this means there is effectively no limit to the fetch, so nothing to stop waves building. In reality, they rarely exceed 80ft.

The ocean's breadth exceeds 1,200 miles throughout, except at Cape Horn. Here, where South America extends to almost 56°S and Graham Land, part of Antarctica, reaches north to 60°S, the width is 240 miles. The ocean pours through this channel on its way east, propelled by the prevailing westerly winds. The wide 'river' accelerates at this point and shallow banks further constrict it, which explains the area's big seas. And to add to a sailor's woes, the temperature of much of the area is little above freezing.

Unaffected by land, the surface wind is basically created by high pressure to the north and low-pressure systems to the south that move eastwards through the ocean. In the northern section the winds are largely westerlies, but south of the depressions they are easterlies. Even in summer, 20% of winds are over gale force – far more frequent than is experienced in a northern latitude summer.

The sailor's choice is how far to go into this ocean. To reduce the distance along a Great Circle course, the further south you go, the better, but that means risking going too close to the lows. In any case, it is not possible to make a true Great Circle without crossing the Antarctic, so compromises are necessary.

The safe and traditional route is to keep the high-pressure systems to the north and the low-pressure systems to the south as this guarantees westerly winds. Too far north and winds lighten, too far south and they become too strong and build up seas too large to allow safe, fast sailing.

The ocean is not completely empty. There is a scattering of small islands which are uninhabited apart from small scientific teams. The largest population is on the Kerguelen group, halfway between Africa and Australia at roughly 50°S. Some 2,000 miles from Africa, further still from Australia, and over 1,000 miles from Antarctica, this French-owned outcrop has to be the loneliest continuously manned outpost on Earth. Few days pass when winds of gale force are not recorded here, even in summer.

If the islands are no longer such a hazard because their positions are known and GPS allows accurate navigation in all conditions, icebergs certainly are. Their movement north and quantity varies each year; this year the bergs were mainly at about 60°S, but growlers were sighted 600 miles further north along the 50th parallel.

The image of an ice mountain floating against a clear blue sky is misleading. Mountainous they may be, but they are often hidden in fog, rain or snow and a last-minute crash gybe may be the only way to avoid them.

More hazardous still are the growlers, those lumps that barely break the surface and are harder to see. If icebergs provide a poor radar target, the growlers usually provide none. A full-rigged vessel might be able to push them aside with little more than a bump, but a modern yacht is very vulnerable to a collision and the only real security comes from a good lookout.

The Southern Ocean is a cold, desolate and dangerous region which challenges even the hardest and most experienced seamen – but therein lies its attraction.

ROUND THE HORN
IN A DAY

Cape Horn has a legendary status among sailors, the Mount Everest of sailing, but part of its mystique is the relentless battle across the oceans to get there. A short hop out from the Beagle Channel in December 2008 couldn't count as a real rounding of the Horn, says Robin, but it was fascinating nonetheless.

I f there is an equivalent to Mount Everest for sailors it has to be Cape Horn. But there are shades of achieving Cape Horn. You can sail out from Ushuaia and round it, or you can pass it as a part of a circumnavigation. The sail from the Beagle Channel does not count as a real passage, especially these days when cruise liners make frequent visits. You might just as well sail around Muckle Flugga. It is those wearisome weeks and months surviving the Southern Ocean which is the real challenge and for which the Cape is just the final hurdle before turning north for home.

But how many of the sailors who pass the Horn during their circumnavigation get to explore the island behind it, usually seen as dark and rather forbidding? They are usually hurrying on from Tierra del Fuego and even this rocky and rugged coastline seems to flinch eastwards away from the relentless battering of the Southern Ocean. And yet the chart shows an enticing maze of fjords just begging to be explored behind Isla Hornos.

I sailed into the Beagle Channel in 2007 to repair my communication systems. It was dark, blowing close to 40 knots, the top slide on the mainsail had broken, the drive on my engine was damaged and I was single-handing. It was a nightmare. Thirty-six hours later I departed from Ushuaia, the wind now behind me, and could not help being attracted by the scenery – tall hills and mountains on either side of a channel that seldom exceeds three miles in width, but narrowing to half a mile in places and, best of all, very few signs of habitation. I knew I wanted to come back, but not in an Open 60 with its kelp-catching keel!

In December my wishes were granted when I joined Skip Novak aboard his yacht *Pelagic*, with special permission from the Chilean Navy to sail out of the western end of the Beagle Channel via Bahia Cook. Most of Tierra del Fuego is Chilean and it is their Navy that controls the waterways and with whom one must clear inwards, usually at Puerto Williams, about 25 miles east from Ushuaia. There is a small sheltered creek to the west of the town where the yachts moor, but once cleared we headed out again to the west.

The wind here has its quiet spells – we found we often had a few hours in the morning when it was quite light – but it soon got back to its normal 30-plus knots. But there are sheltered anchorages tucked away and known to those who sail here most years and these proved safe and attractive, once the anchor(s) held and lines had been put out ashore. These are usually only a few hours' motor sailing apart, far enough to make reaching them a relief, but close enough so they can be reached within a few hours.

We saw glaciers falling into the sea, picked up crab's legs from local fishermen, had a barbecue with a whole sheep and wondered how

Captain Fitzroy had managed to explore these waters in a square rigger in 1833. As we sailed south through Bahia Cook, we slowly began to feel the effects of the Southern Ocean swell, but the wind was behind us and we reached fast out to sea and then gybed eastwards.

Even though the Beagle Channel was a fascinating cruising ground and one I would like to visit again, the highlight of the trip was not heading out into the Southern Ocean, but landing on Isla Hornos. Most people sail straight past this Cape, thankful to put it behind them. We sailed passed the Cape itself about half a mile off, much closer than I would usually care to go, but conditions were perfect for a close look. Then we turned north up its east coast and into the Wollaston Archipelago. If we had hoped for photos of huge seas breaking over the point, we were disappointed as the wind was about a Force 3 and the sea calm, apart from the endless swell.

The island is manned. It has a Chilean petty officer and his family in a nice new house which is resupplied every two months. They run the two lights and the radio station and host the occasional visitor, who can land in a bay on the south-east corner and take the steps up to the cliff.

This was an interesting visit, but in my book does not count as a real rounding of the Cape.

PART SEVEN

Sailing and the Wider World

SAILING AND THE MEDIA

In Robin's first column for *Yachting World* in January 1993 he put the case for more coverage of our sport by responsible journalists – and not to add the tag 'luxury' every time they used the word 'yacht'.

Next to one's own television show, a column must be the equivalent of having one's own pulpit. Thus, when the Editor asked me whether I would like to sound off in print on a monthly basis, the invitation was irresistible. Like everything else in life, though, there are natural checks and balances – if members of the congregation don't like the sermon, they won't come to church!

Bernard Hayman, who edited *Yachting World* for many years and used to write a column, has been a friend for a long time. We first met when I returned from sailing non-stop around the world 23 years ago. I was able to thank him personally for being one of the very few journalists who had said before I set out that I might succeed in what was then an untried venture. Bernard, like myself, had a Merchant Navy background, and he knew the unbeatable training in seamanship and navigation taught to apprentices during their four years' indentures.

This does not mean we have always seen eye to eye on matters nautical. Perhaps our greatest disagreements were over single-handed sailing. Bernard maintained that it was inherently unsafe and broke Rule 5 of the International Regulations requiring a vessel to keep a proper lookout at all times, whereas I do not consider it unsafe, if done sensibly.

Apart from the viewpoint of such specialised and experienced journalists, yachting is not considered to be a media sport – and certainly not suitable for television, or so I am constantly being informed by representatives of that industry. One can argue that the French, Australians and Americans seem to be able to make yacht racing a mass spectacle, but we are then told that their television is not as good as ours!

The result is that, apart from the occasional excellent coverage from regional stations, we have only BBC Radio 4's *Waterlines* once a week for 16 weeks a year. So our poor minority sport (there are only a few million of us) is forced to depend on magazines and short newspaper columns to provide the only effective link between the various branches of yachting.

Here is the nub of the problem. People – and journalists in particular – do not grasp the point that yachting is as broad-based as, say, athletics. They also seem incapable of mentioning the word 'yacht' without prefixing it with the word 'luxury', a cause of raucous laughter among many sailing families.

But does it really matter? It can be claimed that sailors belong to the genus participant rather than spectator, and most of us go to sea to escape the crowds. It is only a small number of sailors seeking sponsorship who need publicity and thus suffer from the lack of media attention.

In fact, we do lose out as a result because 20 years ago the British boating industry was the undoubted leader in Europe. Across the Channel in France, however, after Eric Tabarly had won the OSTAR, things were beginning to happen. An hour-long, year-round, weekly yachting programme started and demand for boats rose – just as our industry was knocked sideways by the imposition of a punitive 25% VAT.

Jeanneau and Bénéteau expanded to a point where they dominated sailing boat production. Races were organised to suit the French media and these events emphasised the new equipment and techniques that their industry had produced.

Not every British company lost out, of course; some still held their positions, but in general the leader was now France. I can remember being told by a well-known British sailmaker that my multihull did not require flat sails since multihulls do not go to windward. He had not been watching the French or he would have realised that, with the right sails, multihulls give as good a windward performance as any monohull.

Publicity does help a sport. It expands the demand for its products and increases competition and choice. It also gives political clout. Can you imagine the politicians daring to apply a 25% VAT rate on football? And to what extent was the greedy rise in berthing rates on the South Coast due to politicians refusing to allow more berthing?

It was 'green' and therefore safe to refuse planning applications for more marinas to berth 'luxury' yachts, owned (of course) by yuppies. That perception is very far from the truth, but until we start acquiring a more sympathetic image for yachting, the truth will not be a vote winner.

VIEW FROM THE BRIDGE

Robin had a good view of how yachts dealt with the traffic rules from the deck of the *QE2* in 1994. In the main, he was not greatly impressed by his fellow yachtsmen.

Motoring up the Solent at 18 knots on a large liner puts a new perspective on the meaning of a close quarters situation. What no doubt appears to be a safe distance from the cockpit of a yacht looks dangerously close from the bridge of the *QE2*, but the most concern was caused by boats whose movements were difficult to interpret – those which were heading straight across the path or angling diagonally to cross it.

The *QE2* is 70,000 tons and is not able to swerve to avoid something close ahead and, as the Captain pointed out (and he is a yachtsman), even if she did alter course, it would only threaten other small vessels to one side or the other which had been clear up to that point.

My immediate assumption was that yachtsmen were not aware of the local bye-laws covering shipping in the Solent area, but examination of the log of the accompanying safety vessel indicated otherwise.

Most boats that were challenged admitted that they had heard that there were rules although not all knew the details. Excuses given for getting in the way divided pretty evenly between:

"I was well clear" (in one case from a yacht 100m in front of an approaching container ship when the moving exclusion zone extends 1,000m ahead!).

"The ship was going faster than I realised and I thought I had time to get across".

"The wind went light" (so use your motor please, sir!).

"I'm sorry".

For those 35,000 yachts that habitually use the Solent, there are some significant points to be appreciated. The first is that most of the ships coming out of the Port of Southampton, except the large tankers, only slow down at Prince Consort buoy if coming from the east, and almost at Calshot Spit if from the Needles.

They need to keep speed on in order to turn sharply at these two points and, once committed, cannot manoeuvre out of the way of yachts in the channel. Every yachtsman knows that if they want to turn sharply they need to put on high revs to direct a good wash against the rudder – well, this applies to giants as well.

The safety boats that now accompany vessels coming through the channels will tow becalmed yachts out of the way, but they rely on the intelligence and watchfulness of other boats to keep well clear. If there are a number of yachts becalmed in the channel there is going to be trouble, since there just won't be time to get to them all.

A classic case of this was when the offshore racing fleet was becalmed and many kedged right in the channel, in the centre of the zone of concern. The container ship coming through had a simple choice: hit four ahead or three astern. It took the cheaper alternative!

There were, no doubt, some indignant yachtsmen as a result, but they only have themselves to blame. A tight dredged channel into a busy principal port is hardly an intelligent place to anchor and this is a clear example of where the Rules of the Road take precedence over the racing rules.

Surprisingly, on average, only three are hit each year, or perhaps that should be put the other way round, as on two occasions recently the yachts have rammed the ships. One was a sailing school boat which went bow first into the ship's side; the other was a small cruiser, out for the first time with new owners who could not get their engine started quickly enough.

They bounced down the side, damaging hull and rigging in the process, and were lucky to avoid serious difficulties at the stern where the propellers create a suction. Either way, it was a sad start to their new ownership.

This happened on a Sunday in early October, so the Solent was only moderately busy; it must be a nightmare during Cowes Week. The port authorities do have the power to take to court owners who flout the rules, but this has been used very sparingly so far.

If yachtsmen don't want a rash of summonses, the rule has to be: if you see a large vessel coming up the channel, get clear of the zone of concern in good time. It is both considerate and common sense – in other words, good seamanship.

JUST FOR KICKS

Sailing across the Atlantic in a bottle or swimming next to a raft – are these stunts really tests of bravery and skill, or just irresponsible publicity bashes, putting lives on the line?

I find it difficult to come down with a firm view on stunts in yachting – stunts being defined as anything out of the ordinary and slightly dangerous in boating terms.

Sailing the Atlantic in ever smaller craft, motoring across in bottles, windsurfing, rowing, crossing in a pedalo and in now what is claimed to be the first transatlantic swim all fit into the category, as does someone with no seagoing experience setting out in an unsuitable craft.

Part of me admires the courage of those concerned, another part worries whether they know what they are doing. The final part is concerned about the unnecessary risks taken by lifesaving volunteers if things go wrong, either in large vessels diverted for the purpose or the lifeboatmen. Is it responsible?

Well, can any sport that involves risk be justified? Surely this depends upon the thought put into safety preparations and the degree of danger involved.

For example, I was not particularly taken by a mountaineer's excuse after the rescue team failed to find yet another missing climber in Scotland earlier this year. His justification for the risks being taken was that rescue teams enjoyed having a call-out.

Perhaps they do. Perhaps they train hard and keep themselves on 24-hour standby just for the vicarious thrill of seeing if they can recover a missing climber before they die. However, expressed like this, it sounds like some advanced form of video game or the lottery, and reduces the value of a life to a shabby score. I am sure lifesavers do relish the challenge, but I am also certain that, in reality, the selfless and professional way they put their own lives at risk to help others has a deeper motivation.

One of the essences of good seamanship is safety, so are the stunts justifiable? Well, Frenchman Guy Delage apparently swam across the Atlantic pushing a raft which contained all the necessities for his existence, including a fax machine. The machine enabled him to be in touch with the media, send back his reports and keep publicity rolling.

It is reported that he drifted more than he swam and one can imagine that as the public interest increased, the pressures from the media will have meant that even the daily average of eight or so hours spent swimming would have to be reduced – one has to get the priorities right in these matters!

Spending 16 hours a day drifting on a glorified sunbed is not exactly what I would call swimming the Atlantic, but if it were to be attempted without the props we all know it would be impossible. The performance proved nothing except perhaps that the currents will eventually push you westwards if you attempt to cross the Atlantic level with the Canary Islands. This has been known since the times of the Phoenicians, was proved by Columbus and nowadays there are better and more efficient methods to discover how the oceanic currents work.

Delage knows a thing or two about stunts and publicity. I raced against him across the Atlantic in the 1982 Route du Rhum when he was sailing a small proa. He graduated from that to an enormous one called *Rosières,* which was a Meccano enthusiast's dream.

It had a pod that could wiggle around, which fascinated journalists and the public alike and attracted huge attention prior to the race. It drew even more when it collapsed as it was towed to the start line.

This delighted the sponsor, as the break-up took place on a Saturday afternoon, live on TV, and gained more publicity than the race itself. Delage satisfied his sponsor without even starting the race. After such a striking success he could have been expected to reappear fairly quickly with something even more futuristic, though it has taken him more than 10 years to come up with the raft.

Whether you consider the raft responsible and safe or not, the media loved it and it even pushed the first Englishman to walk in space off the front pages of some of our newspapers. While stunts can achieve success like that in newspaper column inches, people are bound to be encouraged to do them.

MEN BEHAVING BADLY

When an England football player punched his wife in 1996, Robin was horrified that the perpetrator could carry on representing his country. Sailors are much better role models, he believes.

I f we, as a nation, are to be judged abroad by our sportsmen, the time has come to cease referring to soccer as the national game. The hugely publicised, loutish behaviour of one of the England players just goes to show what can happen when people who are protected and cosseted from the realities and responsibilities of real life – by no doubt well-meaning, but seriously misguided managers – are given the attention they don't deserve and cannot handle.

Punching one's wife could be considered a private matter if the wife does not object, but she would have to be a pretty poor creature not to. However, when it is done by someone who is almost daily in the newspapers, it sends out signals about our society that I hope are wrong and I certainly don't want publicised.

The bully boy – because in my old-fashioned way that is what I call someone who abuses his or her strength deliberately to hurt someone smaller and weaker – acts humble and says he is having counselling. Counselling is used in these modern times as the all-embracing palliative when anything that requires a bit of character has been funked.

So since this person is being counselled, everything is all right and he can go on playing and representing his country at a very high and prominent level. It was a mistaken decision. No one person's career, however gifted, should be preserved if it costs all his countrymen their reputations.

Representing your country is just that: acting as a representative. Once you pull on the uniform you have responsibility to behave with dignity, as well as play your heart out.

It may be only a game, but jobs can depend on the impression our sportsmen and women give. Who wants to buy a product from a country which demonstrates sloppiness? Who treats tourists with respect if their nation's representatives behave like louts?

One hopes that if a yachtsman were to behave as badly, the national authority would not hesitate to impose a long ban as a punishment as they have in the past. The football authorities, by dodging the issue, have shown that their prima donnas can break all the normal rules in society and get away with it.

That is no example to show our youth. Being a familiar name to the public may bring some privileges, but it also brings responsibilities and that is the message that is lacking from football.

Compare our footballer with our Olympic rowers and sailors – high-spirited from time to time, I would hope, but not pictured in the papers as unable to provide normal standards of balanced, civilised behaviour.

Look at Pete Goss, who set out in November 1996 in the Vendée Globe Challenge, which is without question the toughest yacht race in the world. He is a skilled sailor, proudly flying his country's flag in a major international event. He is not surrounded by sycophants, daily flattering his ego; he is alone, quietly facing up to the unforgiving ocean without help, largely unnoticed by the media, and with the added pressure of a massive overdraft.

You would not hesitate a nanosecond if you had to choose a companion for some really dangerous or difficult adventure or one that required real toughness; the footballer would not even appear in my top 10,000.

If sportsmen are going to be seen as representatives of our society, then let's have the likes of our young Olympic sailors or Pete Goss as our standard bearers – though as individual yachtsmen and women we are not immune from this responsibility. Hoisting the red, white or blue ensign is no different from putting on the national jersey.

Bad behaviour, selfish actions, poor boat handling all lead people to look for the ensign and refer to "that **** Brit". The next boat in port wonders at their frosty reception until it is learnt that they are judged by a fellow countryman's standards – just as a well-behaved English football supporter finds himself herded like an animal by foreign police because others have behaved badly.

BATTLE OF THE BOOKS

Which has the greatest wealth of literature, sailing or mountaineering? Well, sailing, of course, declares Robin, especially if you count all the seafaring tales from the great days of sail.

"Of course, sailing does not have the wealth of literature of mountaineering," declared Chris Bonington as he hauled in the slack while I pulled myself up to him.

We were ascending the Cathedral, a previously unclimbed mountain in Greenland and his remark nearly caused me to let go in surprise.

I have always considered that the sea has a huge and rich reservoir of writing, while I had seen little of mountain literature except for the obvious books by Chris and those about the conquest of Everest.

We argued amicably for the next couple of hours, as we worked our way higher, the strength of my arguments lying in the fact that Chris did not really know anything about maritime literature, but I was equally weak on mountaineering.

The Bible, usually such a fruitful source of examples, does not appear to take sides because, although the ancient prophets obviously felt the call of the mountains (since they were always disappearing up them for some peace and quiet or to harangue their followers), St Paul provides us with the earliest credible account of a shipwreck on Malta on his way to Rome as a prisoner.

Noah is, of course, the classic sailor/mountaineer, performing a voyage that finished on the summit of Mount Ararat and, by showing how suitable boats are for such expeditions, placing one foot squarely in each camp.

Which sport could claim the legendary explorer HW Tilman took us at least half an hour to decide, Chris winning on the basis that Tilman had become famous as Shipton's climbing partner long before he was known as a sailor.

Since that conversation I have checked bookshops to see which of us was right and have come to the conclusion that, even if yachting were not the stronger on its own, the sea would win hands down.

Yachting can claim to be just a small part of an enormous wealth of maritime literature covering everything from battles, trade exploration to adventure, and has spawned some brilliant fiction.

The average yachtsman's interest in the marine environment extends beyond the confines of the sport alone into matters of the sea in all its forms.

Yachting has made a considerable contribution to this library, starting with the first of the genre of sailing accounts, McMullen's *Down Channel*, published 150 years ago, through classics like Slocum's *Sailing Alone Around the World*, and *The Riddle of the Sands*, to the enormous choice of books being published today.

Although the earliest sea story in English must be *Beowulf*, our maritime literature really starts in the nineteenth century, a period when sea voyages were still risky enough to be considered daring and therefore romantic.

Richard Henry Dana and Herman Melville wrote their classics, *Two Years Before the Mast* and *Moby Dick*, in the first half of the nineteenth century. Both are American authors, of course, but the English language whose spread may legitimately be claimed to have started with Cabot's voyage to Newfoundland in *The Matthew* 500 years ago, owed its radiation and subsequent consolidation to the spread of English colonies around the world and their mutual communication by means of the sea.

This being the case, it would be surprising if there were not a wealth of good stories involving the sea emanating from those English-speaking countries that share the same seafaring traditions.

Eric Newby has given us *The Last Grain Race* and, on the fictional front, CS Forester and Patrick O'Brian write rattling yarns. These works are probably the most appreciated by seafarers who have the benefit of some technical knowledge, thus making the detail in the story more interesting.

SAFE TO SET SAIL?

It isn't always easy to explain to a non-sailor why you postpone the start of a race because of bad weather when the boats are likely to be meeting equally bad weather, if not worse, on their ocean crossings. But the dangers of a lee shore, confused seas and even getting out of the marina safely weigh heavily, explains Robin.

"What I don't understand," said the interviewer, "is that these are ocean-going yachts; they have to cope with just as bad conditions out at sea, so why can't they leave port on schedule?"

It is a question that was raised a number of times in October 2002 when bad weather forced us to cancel, by a day each time, the start of both the second leg of the Around Alone single-handed race from Torbay and the first leg of the Clipper Round the World Race from

Liverpool. Yes, the boats would have to cope with such conditions out at sea, so what was the problem?

For sailors the answer isn't difficult. At sea you have room to manoeuvre. If bad conditions do develop, you can snug the boat down and it doesn't matter where you drift until the storm passes, because you are unlikely to hit anything. Sending boats out to sea from a safe port is a different matter.

The land is an immediate restriction, removing at least half the drift options. The seas are usually more disturbed – not as big maybe, but more likely to be confused with the shallower water and reflected waves returning from adjacent land.

In any case, it's often the waves found close to land that are the most difficult to deal with in a small boat.

Above all, there's the risk that if anything goes wrong there is a lee shore lying close by and options are becoming very limited.

It does not matter if the mainsail is torn, a halyard jammed or the engine won't start when there is plenty of room to drift; they can all be dealt with later. But they can be life-threatening when there are only hours before the draught exceeds the depth of water.

Time after time the conclusions reached in reports from the Marine Accident Investigation Branch (MAIB) is that once one thing goes wrong, you must rethink the plan to take into account the more limited options. Bad weather is one thing that can go wrong.

In the case of the two race postponements, the real problem was going to be to get the boats safely out of the marinas. Very heavy gusts – 90-plus knots in the Liverpool area, over 70 at Berry Head – meant that the wind was taking charge. The boats could not guarantee to be under control in a heavy gust and damage would be an almost certain result.

With damage comes the risk of injury to crews. Postponement was, therefore, the only recourse. A day late in sailing is not particularly important when the races are lasting the best part of a year, so trying to start them and risking serious damage could mean a participant being put out of the event.

It was not a popular decision in either case. While the sailors and professionals were supportive and relieved, PR people and sponsors were horrified at the thought of their important guests not being able to witness the start they had given up their time to watch.

For these people, the fact that on each occasion trees were being blown over, power lines were down, large ships were heading for shelter or not moving and trains were being stopped was not a sufficient reason for cancellation.

The uproar was deafening and you would have thought it the worst crisis ever. Forget Wimbledon being rained off, cricket matches delayed, or football cancelled due to heavy frost, for some reason this was a far greater crisis.

Well, yes, it could have been, had we tried to start on the appointed days.

MEDALS AND THE MEDIA

As the Beijing Olympics approached, the medal chances of our sailing team looked very bright indeed, but Robin asks what will it take for the non-yachting media to notice and take pride in our sailors?

I think time must speed up as we get older. It doesn't seem like three years since the last Olympics, but here we are again in 2008 selecting a team for next year in Qingdao. Listening to the radio, you could be forgiven for thinking that sailing was not an Olympic sport and, unfortunately, the non-yachting media tends to treat sailing as a peripheral minority interest.

Well, let's just remind ourselves that sailing was Britain's best medal winner in 2000 and 2004 and, furthermore, Britain came top of the sailing medal table in both those Olympics.

It seems to have gone unnoticed that in the pre-Olympics in Qingdao this year the British team won five Golds and a Silver medal out of a possible haul of 11 medals. Compare that with the coverage of the less than impressive athletics team in Beijing who potentially compete for more than 60 medals.[1]

Our sailors punch well above their weight, but the media exposure they get is well below what it should be. This affects our sport's ability to source public funds for major facilities. Football, which is hardly short of money, received £120 million towards the new Wembley Stadium from the Lottery. Rowing, a successful sport for the United Kingdom, but not as successful as sailing, receives far more support – why is it that the British seem to excel in the waterborne sports? The Navy used to be known as the Silent Service, but there is no need for sailing to maintain this tradition.

So our preparations are going well and we just have to hope that we do not peak too early, or become over-confident. For the Kingston Olympics in Canada in 1976 we sent a team of world champions, but came back with just Reg White's Gold medal in the Tornado catamaran, so there is a danger of over-confidence. That is why I wonder whether we are choosing our team rather too early. There is a case for saying that early selection enables a crew to concentrate on their preparations, but I am not convinced that those preparations would not be better made if the crews still had to compete until closer to the actual regatta.

The pressure tends to focus people's minds, in my experience, and there is no way of knowing whether the chosen crew will be at their best in, say, six months' time, or someone else will have improved sufficiently to make a serious challenge to them. What matters is who will be at their best, and at world-beating best, in Qingdao next year. As a sport we do need a thumping success in the 2008 Olympics, so we can use it as a stick with which to beat the TV media and grab their attention.

Meanwhile, plans for the development of our sailing Olympics centre in Weymouth are progressing nicely. It is due to open in August 2010, giving plenty of time to get bedded in before the 2012 Games. Ever since the sailing academy opened in the old naval port, it has seen increased usage by our dinghy sailors. Yet its full potential development

---

[1] Note: In the event Britain won four Golds, one Silver and one Bronze medal at the Beijing Olympics.

would not have been achieved for some time if the Olympics had not come along, as the money was just not forthcoming.

We can all benefit from this development. Portland is already developing as a yachting centre and the Olympics can only hasten this. The new marina will take pressure off the moorings in the town – much as many of us enjoy rafting up there, the increase in yachting has meant that the trots have grown ever wider.

Whatever the doubts about the weather conditions in China, Weymouth should give no worries on that score. Compared with alternative sites, it has some huge advantages. The most important one is that Weymouth Bay, north of Portland Bill, is relatively tideless, unlike the Solent or the Thames. It is a perfect site for a large regatta as there is plenty of space to lay out a large number of courses.

Add to this the shelter Portland gives from the waves that can sweep up the Channel, and the fact that there is space in Portland Harbour to build first-class shore facilities.

We have the site, it will have the facilities and we are very strong internationally in the sport. We just need people outside sailing to appreciate this and share the pride those of us who sail have in our Olympic sailors.

ELF AND SAFETY

When Health and Safety want us to put safety rails around finger pontoons and insist that a Topper dinghy must carry a liferaft, it would be laughable if it wasn't so serious. We need rules made by people who understand that the sea is a law unto itself, says Robin.

I t is hard to create rules that can deal with the unpredictable and the sea is unpredictable. It is not conducive to bureaucratic rules and the seaman's task is to be aware and prepared for the vagaries that nature can throw.

That is why the Health and Safety Executive (HSE) has such difficulties with anything maritime. If they create a rule that gives them a box to tick, which absolves them from further responsibility, the sea tends to come up with a problem that is outside the confines of the box. This, of course, makes them even more cautious.

160

This is not the only problem we sailors have with the health and safety industry. Officials tend to dictate rules without knowing what they are for. Often they do not have the background knowledge of the subject and as a result become more dogmatic (or arrogant) as a defensive posture.

That's not to say we don't need rules. We do, to cover safety at sea. But we need them made by people who understand the situation and can make decisions based on what suits a very practical environment, not by those who produce a rule book and protect themselves behind its contents.

There are some frightening examples of the bureaucrat at work: the HSE official who said that a Topper dinghy must carry a liferaft, for example; or one who demanded safety rails around finger pontoons, completely missing the point that a crew member who jumped ashore with a mooring line would be bruised or knocked back into the water when they hit this 'safety' rail.

Or how about the demand that all commercial yachts must carry a body bag for every member of the crew. Presumably the zip on the last one would be inside the bag, so the final survivor could close it with their dying gasp. Then there was the statement that bodies in body bags on commercial yachts should be stored in a refrigerator until the next port, overlooking that a 60ft yacht doesn't have a refrigerator anywhere near large enough.

The BBC issued a diktat that staff going on a boat for the first time must do a sea survival course, most of which would be bewildering. What they needed was to become familiar with a boat, so they might understand the detail of the course. But the course provided a box that could be ticked, even though it was akin to teaching a pilot how to deal with a crash before teaching them how to fly. The same BBC person asked for a Port Safety Certificate for a boat, unaware of the MCA coding system. A request for details of exactly what was a Port Safety Certificate led to a deafening silence.

Berthon Boat Company in Lymington had a visit from Health and Safety inspectors and was ordered to put a safety rail around the inside of staging in their paint spray shed. The staging abuts the boat anyway, but that was not acceptable within the rules. It was pointed out that this would make painting impossible, but the response was that if they did not follow these instructions they would be closed down. Fortunately, an appeal to higher authority reversed the demand.

The horrors go on, but all reflect stupidity at best, the arrogant abuse of power at worst. It all costs time and money, an unnecessary expense to industry which gets passed on to the customer and the theft of our valuable leisure time. These examples would be laughable if they were not so serious. But maybe we ought to be doing more laughing. Ridicule is a powerful weapon and stupid decisions by petty bureaucrats ought to be challenged as a matter of principle.

The world is becoming far too full of these negative and time-wasting people. A poem by Shel Silverstein sums up how we should react:

> Listen to the mustn'ts, child
> Listen to the don'ts
> Listen to the shouldn'ts, the impossibles, the won'ts
> Listen to the don't haves, then listen close to me
> Everything is possible, anything can be.

If every child was forced to understand this, we could get moving. Every bureaucrat ought to be made to feel frightened of being called a 'mustn't'.

KNITTLES AND BOMKINS

If you've ever said you were 'taken aback' or there'd be 'the devil to pay' did you know these are nautical expressions, many of which are being lost? Robin loves the rich and dynamic lexicon of the sea.

I am an avid collector of nautical words and expressions. The habit began around 40 years ago and in the intervening period I have noted down any new word I have come across, searched out its meaning and written it down.

Many of these words are no longer in use – you rarely hear anyone talk about 'wooldings' when they are putting a seizing around a sprung mast to hold it together, but this seems natural. Wooden masts have largely been replaced by aluminium or carbon fibre and although a form of lashing might work to bind a modern mast, it is unlikely.

'Amain' is another lost term, but far more useful – it means to let go a rope and allow it to run freely. Or there are 'bomkins', two pieces of timber that extend from the sides of the stem to allow the fore tacks to be hauled down. It sounds similar to bumkins, which we still use, but to describe something that extends from the stern to allow a sheet to be secured abaft the hull.

How many of us nowadays would walk into a chandlery and ask for 'a knittle' to refer to a length of small-diameter cord, or use a 'nun-buoy', an anchor buoy which consists of a barrel attached to the anchor to show where it is lying? 'Lurching' is what we would call a knockdown when the boat is suddenly forced onto her side by a squall.

One term that many sailors may recognise is 'to wear', by which is meant going from one tack to the other by turning away from the wind instead of putting the bow into the wind. It is often referred to as gybing, but if you are going from hard on the wind on one tack to hard on the wind on the other, you have weared.

'Gazinta' is a Merchant Navy term for a dog's-leg brush because it 'gets inta' places a normal brush can't. Another Merchant Navyism is to 'ease' a cable; the Royal Navy 'veers' it just to cause confusion. To 'borrow' is to sail towards an object, but not get too close. The 'baboon watch' is the one in which a junior member of the crew is left on deck while everyone else goes below. A 'banyan day' is one in which no meat is served in the crew's meals.

Many of the seaman's expressions have come ashore, but few people appreciate their origins. 'The devil to pay' is one of the more obvious – the devil, the outermost seam in the ship's deck, was notoriously hard to caulk and pay with pitch. This also explains the meaning of being 'between the devil and the deep blue sea' – hanging overside. 'Letting the cat out of the bag' – disclosing information unwittingly – derives from removing the cat-o-nine-tails from a bag for punishment.

Other phrases are more obscure. 'Slush fund' has come to mean a fund of money collected to be used for some nefarious purpose. In fact, it originates from a sea cook's perk. When meat was cooked for the crew's meal, the excess fat was carefully collected and was the cook's to sell, often to the purser to use for making candles or for greasing blocks or masts, so that the parrels could slide more easily.

'Taken aback' has come ashore as well, usually to express surprise, but it originally refers to a situation in which the wind suddenly changes direction and fills the sails from the forward side, thereby stopping a

164

vessel's forward momentum. It was a dangerous situation because it put the weight of the sails onto the forestays such as the mainbrace.

'Hand over fist' referred to the action of hauling on a halyard or of seamen climbing aloft, but has come to mean paying too much for something. If anyone can explain how that change came about, then please let me know.

The language of the sea is rich and dynamic. The English version has contributions from the United States, Australia, New Zealand and the West Indies, most of which are shared. There are exceptions: 'gerdunk', the US Navy term for what we would call the NAAFI shop, is particularly American and refers to the noise made by a can of Coca-Cola coming out of a dispensing machine.

Throughout history new words have been added to the nautical lexicon as new inventions arrive. Conversely, as technology takes over the task previously done by something else, the old word falls into disuse and will eventually be forgotten. Or recorded somewhere, hopefully.

PART EIGHT

Hazards of the Oceans

ENZA'S UFO

When Robin's multihull *ENZA New Zealand* struck an unidentified floating object in the Southern Ocean while chasing the outright round the world record in 1993, the press decided it was a container – which was news to the crew. . .

All three of the Jules Verne contestants have now hit something at sea and sustained damage. When we struck something in the Southern Ocean aboard *ENZA New Zealand*, the first reports we received stated that we had hit a submerged container.

The truth is we have no idea what we hit. The incident occurred towards midnight and we did not see anything. However, the press automatically assumed that it was a container and went so far as to state that it was floating "just below the surface of the sea".

Now, I don't know how familiar with Archimedes' principles the average reader of *Yachting World* is, but it must be pretty obvious that for an object to 'float' just below the surface requires the maintenance of a million to one coincidence.

Commodore Lane Fox, Flag Officer Submarines, told me that submariners would love to know how to balance an object at a set depth – the way they do it is to keep some momentum and maintain depth with hydroplanes. Objects are usually heavier or lighter than the volume of water they displace. To be the exact weight requires a miracle of balance almost impossible close to the sea's surface – the pressure changes with each passing wave.

So it is extremely unlikely we struck a container floating just below the surface. What is far more probable is that we collided with a large log – we saw plenty from the Bay of Biscay onwards. Whales, too, are a possibility, since they do seem to have developed bad hearing in recent years, judging by the number of collisions claimed with them, not least the third and last contestant in the Jules Verne Trophy.

Whales' sonar no longer seems to warn them when a yacht is approaching, although part of the problem is the lack of disturbance and therefore less noise created by a yacht sailing. There are also vastly increased numbers of yachts cruising the oceans of the world, which statistically must increase the possibilities of a collision.

A container cannot be totally ruled out, though, because when filled with some well-packaged cargo, the water is going to take time to seep through the door seals and then through the packaging. While there is still sufficient air within the container to keep it buoyant, it will float, but as the air escapes it will sink lower and lower until it may be awash and extremely hard to see by day, but impossible by night.

At this stage it is a real hazard, not just to small yachts, but to any vessel. Imagine the effect of a modern warship, with its thin hull plating, hitting a container at 30 knots!

How long do containers float around as a serious threat to shipping before sinking? The answer is that no one can tell and it will depend on the cargo anyway, but I was told by a container ship captain that he thought two days would be average – for an empty one.

What is incontrovertible is that if they could be persuaded to sink the moment they fall over the side, a serious danger to shipping would be removed. To this end it is difficult to understand why hydrostatic valves are not fitted to all containers shipped as deck cargo, to allow water into the box the moment it falls overboard. The cost would not be prohibitive; we already fit such valves to liferafts and EPIRBs.

There can be no reason for allowing containers to float around waiting to be recovered, as no one seems remotely interested in salvaging their contents. With underwriters apparently willing to pay up without fuss, no wonder no one bothers, and the Names at Lloyds are suffering!

Long term, the answer must lie in better securing arrangements aboard container ships. Perhaps it is not appreciated that the average metacentric height of such a vessel is 3m, approximately three times that of a similar-sized passenger vessel. This makes them very stiff and as such they will roll more violently.

In turn, this puts additional strain on the container lashings, especially in the higher tiers. Since many container ships rely upon a simple screw lock as a lashing, it is hardly surprising that in a large sea or heavy swell most container ships lose boxes.

Until someone starts making a fuss, it looks as though we shall have to continue to accept the additional risk of hitting a container at sea. There is no point in fitting them with beacons since no one knows how long they will stay afloat, and in any case, taking down reported positions would be a full-time job.

As usual, I suspect it will take a major catastrophe before anyone tackles the problem. In the meantime, expect to pay higher insurance premiums when crossing oceans as you can bet that the insurance industry will not do the logical thing and increase the rates on containers, which might just make people lash them properly and remove the real cause of the problem.

SHADES OF THE *TITANIC*?

Ice has become a hazard as the numbers of yachtsmen sailing across the North Atlantic or round the world increase, especially the low-floating bergs they call growlers.

Sighting ice is not something the average yachtsman who cruises British waters expects, but with an increasing number of yachts crossing the North Atlantic or sailing round the world, ice is becoming a less unusual hazard.

Thus a report that three cargo vessels have been damaged by ice in the North Atlantic this year is of interest – shades of the *Titanic*, except that none of them sank. Apparently they struck growlers, which are defined as occupying an area of about 20 square metres and extending less than a metre above the surface. In practice, they are often just awash, frequently transparent and with 90% of their bulk beneath the surface.

Berg ice is incredibly hard. The really big bergs have broken off from glaciers and have been hundreds of years in the making. This compresses them until they are like rock. I hit one with an ice pick once when desperate to cool some vodka and my wrist and arm rang for a minute – I barely marked the berg.

This sort of ice can and does cut through steel and the faster the vessel is travelling, the more likely it is to be damaged.

The incidents occurred where the Labrador current sweeps down from the Arctic east of Canada, but it is wrong to assume that the bergs will confine themselves to this area. They also drift southward from the east coast of Greenland and have been sighted as far south as 40°N (the latitude of New York or Oporto) and 37°W.

Even in July the ice shelf was at 54°N in 1993, about level with Manchester, and 57°W with bergs sighted at about 44°N, about level with Cape Finisterre. This year has seen ice further south than usual, but it is worth remembering that the traditional liner route from New York to Southampton was along 40°N between 40°W and New York.

For vessels going further north to Halifax, ice was a familiar problem and there was an interesting rule, worth remembering in a yacht, that you never try putting your engines astern when in thick ice. Keeping them in 'slow ahead' allowed most of the ice to drift past, but, if put astern, they dragged the ice into the propeller and damage resulted.

The nearest danger to our waters comes from East Greenland. The pack ice usually seals off most of the coast for all but a couple of months each year, and very large bergs drift southwards past Cape Farvel right through to July/August. I have seen huge bergs in early August just inside the Arctic Circle, but only growlers and brash ice three weeks later.

In winter the Denmark Strait, between Iceland and Greenland, is often reduced to half its width by ice. Fortunately, the waters from the Gulf Stream keep this ice well clear of the UK.

Growlers are the greatest risk. The trouble with them is that they are hard to see and rarely give an echo on the radar. The best indication is a wave that is breaking differently from the general pattern, but this is only possible to see in good visibility. At night there is little chance of seeing anything.

We hit one in the 1977 Whitbread at about 54°S although we had a good lookout posted. Visibility was down to 80ft and by the time the lookout had seen it, we were running over the top. Luckily there was no damage.

During the last BOC solo round the world race with stops, ice was sighted by all the contestants, between 100° and 180°W and as far north as 45°. Earlier this year icebergs were at 44°S in longitude 30°E.

Some boats entered for the 1993 Whitbread race are planning to fit forward-facing echo sounders, which they hope will give advance warning of a large mass in their path, but they are likely to run into definition problems like clutter on a radar. The pitching of the boat won't help either, as the sea's surface will give more spurious echoes.

It's worth a try, though. If they do work, perhaps we can all fit them and avoid hitting containers, logs and the assorted lumps of debris that are floating about the oceans of the world.

TALE OF THE WHALES

Sighting a whale is one of the most exhilarating pleasures of long-distance sailing, so Robin reacts to the announcement in 1994 of a ban on whale hunting south of 40°S with approval.

T hat there should be a whale-hunting-free zone south of latitude 40°S is good news for all seafarers except the very few left who earn their living hunting these great mammals.

One of the greatest pleasures in long-distance sailing is the variety of marine life that will probably be sighted during the voyage. Dolphins and porpoises can appear just about everywhere; flying fish are usual between 30°N and S; sharks are increasingly common. But sighting a whale is the real prize.

Of these creatures, only killer whales are known to attack small boats deliberately. A large shark could cause damage accidentally and whales might become aggressive if they believed the boat was threatening their young, but in general most whale strikes seem to happen by chance.

Whales are not always easy to see, especially when they appear to be sleeping just on the surface in bad light. They melt into the waves. Of course, we have incidents these days, but this is a factor of better communications and the increase in yachts traversing the oceans.

One of my most memorable experiences was sighting a blue whale, the largest animal ever to have lived on Earth, in the South Pacific 25 years ago. It blew about 200 yards from the boat with the noise of a steam locomotive. It was an awesome sight and I was naturally concerned: it was three times the length of *Suhaili* and 10 times heavier.

Sadly, my chances of seeing one of these wonderful creatures are very slight, since the numbers are now estimated to be less than 1,000 and one organisation put it as low as 450. One would be distressed if they, and other whales, were dying out through some incurable disease, but that is not the cause of their plight – it is pure human greed.

Apparently, according to records released in Moscow, the Soviet whaling fleets habitually flouted international agreements concerning controls on numbers, species that could be taken and the hunting seasons and regions, in order to achieve their Commissar-dictated quotas. Since a proper universal annual count was lacking, it went unrecorded that numbers were decreasing to an insupportable level.

Now it may be too late to save some species, the blue being a most likely casualty. Why did this happen when modern technology allows us to produce synthetic alternatives to the parts of the whale that were of commercial use anyway?

As a special dispensation, the Japanese have been allowed to take 350 minke whales a year for what is called 'research purposes'. I don't think it is unreasonable to ask why they need 350 each year; surely one or two would suffice? The answer is, of course, that in fact most end up as delicacies in very expensive Japanese restaurants.

Now I love steak and Dover sole, but I would give up both of these pleasures if beef cattle and sole were threatened with extinction. To make matters worse, the Norwegians are now saying that they will ignore the latest treaty and take 300 minke whales a year as well, half for research, of course!

Both these nations can claim, with some justification, that now there are an estimated three-quarters of a million minke whales, this species is no longer endangered and it should be possible to sustain the numbers while catching enough each year to provide titillation for wealthy Japanese palates. The trouble with this argument is that it is hard to believe any of the whalers would comply with new limits.

While there is no evidence that either nation deliberately breached the rules in the past, all the time the Soviets were helping themselves with a total disregard to the agreements they had signed, there were international observers aboard the Soviet vessels to ensure the rules were enforced. And guess what nationality many of those observers were? If whalers could not be relied upon to restrict themselves before, what makes them trustworthy now?

If the gloomy prognosis for many of the whales turns out to be accurate, then the overkilling will be one of the greatest tragedies to occur this century – and one of the greatest crimes as well.

A CLOSE SHAVE

When a fishing boat converged on Robin off the Shetland Islands in 2000, he thought they were approaching out of curiosity – until he realised that there was no one on watch. . .

I'm alive, but I would have been killed if I hadn't taken last-minute avoiding action. It was like a bad dream. The fishing boat just kept heading towards me, only in the dream the wheel would have refused to move and I would have sat there, hopefully waking before the impact.

The incident occurred when I was abeam of the Shetland Island of Fetlar, some 30 miles north of Lerwick and 15 miles south of Muckle Flugga. Out Skerries were behind me, just visible through the thick mist that had been around since I made a landfall on Sumburgh Head Light early in the morning. The wind was north-north-west Force 4, so I was on port tack.

My thoughts were on dinner and rounding Muckle Flugga that night, but I was enjoying the sight of the bare, windswept hills and could see the waves breaking at the foot of the cliffs. A fishing boat was working to the north-east and another came bustling up from astern, heading in the same direction. Its course was leading it slightly to port of me, but we were converging.

I watched with casual interest as it drew closer. It appeared to alter slightly towards me and I thought it might be closing out of curiosity. On it came until at about 100m away I realised it was not curious, it was on autopilot and was not going to change course. I flung the wheel to starboard and bore away. The speed seemed agonisingly slow, but the port aspect of the fishing boat's hull disappeared and then her bow was level with my stern some eight metres away.

I yelled angrily, but there was no one there to listen. The bridge had windows all around it, but there was no one manning it. As the boat swept past, throwing me around with its bow wave, I could see into the fish deck aft. Like the rest of the deck, it was also deserted. The red-hulled boat was like some *Marie Celeste*, abandoned by her crew and motoring hard towards the Arctic. Only she wasn't abandoned, half an hour later at about 1900, she swung round to the south and began fishing.

Where were the crew? Probably having their supper. I will never know when they had abandoned the bridge. It could have been only momentary, but if that was the case, they should have seen me if they were keeping a proper lookout. I suspect the bridge had been abandoned for a while for the boat to have come so close to me. I doubt they even knew I existed. If I had not been at the helm I would have been run down and they might not have noticed – it was quite a large boat.

For this very reason I have always been worried when people talk about sending large merchant ships across oceans unmanned. What intelligence on board is going to make those last-minute alterations to course or speed to avoid a calamity? Yachtsmen have as much right as anyone to use the seas and as much right to expect the same consideration as everyone else.

With that must go the responsibility to give the same consideration you expect from others. Yes, I was single-handing, but that is immaterial since I was on watch and keeping a good lookout. My last sleep had been a snatched hour in the cockpit at 0300 that morning and I was not to rest again for a further 10 hours until I was well west of the

Shetlands – self-preservation dictated I had to be alert that close to land. However, at worst, my six-ton yacht would have inconvenienced a 100-ton fishing boat. It could have killed me.

Regrettably, this incident is not unusual and it behoves yachtsmen, out of sheer self-preservation, to be wary of fishing craft around our coast. Even when not fishing, they must comply with the same rules as the rest of shipping.

I reckon there is a Shetland fishing skipper who owes me a very large bottle of decent malt.

THAR SHE BLOWS!

Never mind containers, striking a whale or a large fish can severely cripple a yacht. And often they don't seem to hear you coming. . .

Perhaps it is because far more yachts are making long passages, but we seem to hear many more incidents of yachts striking objects at sea. Five out of the 11 yachts that completed the Cape Town to Tauranga leg of Around Alone in 2003 struck something and two lost rudders as a result.

With an estimated 10,000 containers being lost at sea each year, the fear of hitting one is now very real. It is thought most containers float for about three months before their contents become waterlogged and the air trapped inside, usually in packaging, escapes. A container that is just awash, when it still has some buoyancy left, is most dangerous because it is not easy to see in daylight and impossible to spot at night.

However, containers are less likely in the Southern Ocean. In all cases, so far as the Around Alone skippers could ascertain, the objects struck were fish or mammals. Since the boats were brought to a complete standstill on each occasion, they were not small either. You would think a fish or mammal would hear the boat approaching but, clearly, this does not always happen. If a boat is not using its engine and does not have a generator running, the only sound to alert anything in the water is something like the echo sounder. But if you go swimming when the echo sounder is on, can you hear it?

Some animals do not hear a boat approaching even with an engine running. I was able to sidle right up alongside a 20ft basking shark in the Firth of Clyde with the engine just ticking over and it only reacted when our shadow came over it. The reaction was quite dramatic. A 5ft tail emerged right by the bow and struck the bowsprit guys, which set the whole rig jangling.

And aboard a large passenger liner, we noticed we had lost half a knot of speed. This could not be accounted for until someone went forward and looked over the bow and discovered a whale, its back broken, caught around the stem. We had to stop and go astern to dislodge it.

Of course, some whales and sharks may approach a yacht out of curiosity, but at least they are aware of your presence; the danger then comes from their not knowing their strength and size. In 1968, when I was sailing across the southern Pacific and was down below making lunch, I suddenly heard what I can only describe as the noise of a steam engine letting off steam. Knowing I was at least 1,000 miles from the nearest land, I leapt on deck. About 200m away a blue whale had surfaced and blown, hence the noise. It must have been close to 100ft in length, so at least 10 times the weight of my boat, and what for it would have been a gentle nudge could have meant a knockdown for me.

So if large fish and mammals cannot always hear a large liner approaching, what chance do they have of sensing a small yacht under sail? It's all a bit of a lottery.

Size aside, the traditional long keelboat is likely to come off better if it hits something close below the surface than a modern lightweight hull with a deep fin keel and suspended rudders. The modern boat is probably going faster for a start, but the long-keeled boat is likely to ride up over the obstruction – a shock for those aboard, but at least the impact is lessened because there is some give. A boat with a fin keel, which probably extends a lot further down and whose hull without the keel has a draught of 2–3ft, will probably hit with this and there is no give at all.

When the strike ratio is as high as 45% of a fleet, it is obviously time we started to consider some means of avoiding the risk posed. Perhaps it is time to invent a fish alarm, working on sound transmissions from the boat, which can alert fish and mammals to a yacht's presence. Of course, it would not work for containers, but maybe they are not the greatest threat.

WAVES THAT DEVOUR SHIPS

In 2003 scientists confirmed as fact what they had long dismissed as mariners' myth – the existence of freak waves. But what can yachtsmen do against a force that is able to disable or sink container ships? asks Robin.

A ccording to my dictionary a freak may be described as a sudden wanton whim or caprice, a vagary. This sums up the appearance of a freak wave pretty well, an occurrence known to mariners, but largely disbelieved by experts ashore. So it was reassuring to watch a BBC programme in which the experts admitted the waves did exist even if they didn't know exactly why.

We can be grateful to the North Sea oil industry for providing evidence of abnormal waves – their fixed platforms provide an unarguable method of measuring wave height. On one, 24 non-linear waves were measured in a four-year period and some exceeded 25m in height. One was measured at 27m when the average wave height was 7m.

About a third of annual merchant ship losses, about 150 ships and 1,200 lives, are put down to adverse weather and it is not just old tonnage that is lost. The *Bremen* was new when she was lost in the Atlantic and *Caledonian Star* was a well-found ship until she was hit by a 30m wave and lost all power. Significantly, she reported a deep trough in front of the wall into which the vessel plunged, thereby exposing her deck.

The linear wave model for ship design is a 15m wave, which is expected to apply a force of 15 tons per square metre. But a freak wave can apply a force of up to 100 tons per square metre, an extreme level not covered by design criteria.

The conditions which led to a freak wave off the south-east coast of South Africa were explained several decades ago. A storm developing south-west of the Cape of Good Hope and travelling eastwards will build up wind and thus seas that run straight into the Agulhas current. This is wind and wave against a four-knot tide (or more) and the effect has been disastrous to those who found themselves exposed.

This type of freak wave can be found wherever a strong current or tide is opposed to a strong wind and wave situation. But this condition does not explain the reports of similar-sized waves in oceans where there is no strong current. A recent survey using radar from satellites found 10 freak waves worldwide within the span of three weeks.

In open oceans, when large waves are being generated, an instability may occur in a group and one wave, perhaps drawing energy from its neighbours, will build up to a height of 26m or more. Large cross-seas can combine to produce a tower of water, such as might be found near a tropical revolving storm or where waves are moving in a different direction from the swell.

Another cause may be a succession of large waves of different frequencies overlapping, as we expect in the Southern Ocean. Significantly, these huge waves frequently have troughs in front of and behind them. The main danger areas are the north-west Pacific, the eastern seaboard of the USA, particularly between Cape Hatteras and the Grand Banks, the north-eastern Atlantic west of the Shetlands and the Southern Ocean.

It will be some time before any official advice is issued about this recently confirmed hazard. And hazard it is – if these waves can overwhelm a container ship and disable passenger ships, imagine what they can do to a yacht. I have only ever experienced one 25m wave. It was in the Southern Ocean and it swept right over the boat. Only the streamed warps prevented us from being broached or rolled and, quite honestly, I cannot remember whether a trough preceded it or not; the wave and its breaking crest had all my attention.

Ocean-going yachtsmen must pay particular attention to their routeing and avoid the danger areas at the dangerous times. We also need to keep a closer watch on the weather, so that if we see something is likely to occur at a certain point in a few days, we can take avoiding action early.

Freak waves are not the only danger and even the Atlantic south of 40°N can create waves of up to 20m in winter. Above all, we need to ensure ocean-going yachts can cope with more dangerous waves than we thought existed.

PART NINE

The Changing Face of Sailing

GOING THE DISTANCE

Robin long resisted the creeping adoption of the 'illogical metric system' for measuring things on boats. But in 1995 he finally gave in and marked out his anchor chain in metres – and he has a lot of chain.

I am not an anti-European. I admire the Germans, like the French, consider the Dutch natural friends and the Portuguese – our oldest ally – delightful.

Ignoring the economists, politicians and bankers, on purely practical grounds I am in favour of the Euro since it will make cruising in Europe so much easier – and anyway, we gave up the farthing and the shilling without a whimper. One common currency will make cruising less expensive too, since it would mean fewer losses in currency exchanges.

The one thing I do object to, however, is the creeping adoption of the illogical metric system for measurements. And what brought all this on, you may ask? Well, it was the reluctant decision to change the markings on my anchor cable from fathoms to metres, since most charts now show depths in this measurement.

I have quite a lot of anchor chain: it is something which it seems stupid to be economical about. When you need security, nothing gives you as much confidence as plenty of heavy cable and a good anchor.

Mine comes in two lots: the first seven fathoms is of five-sixteenths inch and the remaining 21 fathoms of one-quarter inch galvanised chain. The reason for the heavier chain at the anchor is because that is where the most wear takes place and also where one needs the most weight, since no anchor will hold unless the chain is initially lying horizontally along the bottom.

In theory, assuming that I put out the average three times the depth of cable, this amount of chain should enable me to anchor in up to nine fathoms of water (16.452m) in safety, which covers most sensible anchorages.

Of course, to have been really up to date, the change should have been made 28 years ago. The decision to introduce metric units to the range of Admiralty charts came in 1967, at the same time that colours were introduced. More than two-thirds of the well over 3,000 charts now produced by the Hydrographic Department have been converted to metres, so it seemed time to acknowledge the facts.

But why did we have to change? The fathom was so rational – it was my exact armspan, for a start – but 1,000 of them made a nautical mile and 60 of those made a degree and 360 of those got one round the world at the Equator.

There it was, nice and simple and something anyone anywhere in the world could understand. Furthermore, it was already accepted internationally.

Now compare this with the basis of the unChristian kilometre. Originally it was equal to one ten-thousandth of a meridianal quadrant of the Earth, but this was allowed to slip so now it differs considerably from this datum to the point where it is scientifically defined as equal to 1,533,164.13 wave lengths of Red Cadmium light.

It's almost as if they have gone to a complicated figure with decimal points in order to impress us with its precision. The poor simple sailor measured the circumference of the Earth round the Equator as 21,600 of his so-called primitive nautical miles, whereas the scientific metric system has it at a precise 40,075.02 kilometres – which hardly sticks in the mind, does it?

Fortunately, distances are still measured at sea in nautical miles, which links in happily with the units on my sextant, which is just as well, as that would be hard to change. The exporting ability of our electronics industry means that I shall not have to adapt my echo sounder, since metres are already there, but the marks on the hand lead must be altered.

Before they so willingly gave in to the push to metricate us, did any civil servant calculate the real costs in time of the transformation? It may have worked out cheaper to change the side of the road we drive on – something that grieves me much less since ships have traditionally kept to starboard.

Anyway, the deed is done. There are paint marks at every five metres on my anchor chain now so I don't want to read anywhere that we Brits are unwilling Europeans!

ESCAPE TO THE WATER

Overcrowding in tourist areas has become a serious problem on land – just look at the Lake District. So far, we can still escape to sea, but crowded harbours are reducing our free sailing time.

I n one of those rare interviews on BBC Radio 4's *Today* programme that are not interrupted by the presenters, discussion turned to the overcrowding of the Lake District and how visitor numbers might have to be restricted. The arguments ranged from loss of tourist income, now the largest earner in the area, to the damage done to the environment.

I suppose it is inevitable that we shall have to start rationing such attractions sooner or later if we are to preserve them or they will be worn out by the numbers. As a youngster I could freely walk around Stonehenge, but now we all accept we cannot do that if we wish it to survive. This is the price we pay for more leisure time and more discretionary money in our pockets.

Sailing is less damaging to the environment provided crews are careful with their waste. The difference is that the road is an intrusion on the land which has no equal at sea. The only mark of our passing should be the ripple of the wake for a few yards and then the sea will hide our tracks as if we had never been there.

Only when we are close to land do we start to run into similar problems of overcrowding. Too many yachtsmen find it convenient to keep their boats in the same places, which are becoming increasingly crowded.

When you know that to guarantee a berth in, say, Yarmouth you really need to have arrived by the middle of the day, then the purpose in having a boat is beginning to be lost. The boat has become, in practice, little more than a maritime caravan, making short hops between available parks.

The pressure is now on the desirable alternatives. The Solent is becoming so popular that even anchorages like Newtown Creek are no longer the retreats they once were. The East Coast is just as popular; Studland Cove is usually packed at the weekend; Poole and Weymouth have boats five deep; Exmouth and Teignmouth have difficult entrances; Dartmouth and Salcombe are getting busier . . . Two years ago I found it impossible to find a mooring around the Fal, although fortunately there were still some relatively uncrowded anchorages to be had.

The problem facing the sport and the industry is to find places where we can sail at the weekend with the family and give them a night ashore or at least a rest from watchkeeping on Saturday night. It is not that family sailing as a sport has achieved its natural upper limit of participants; it is just that it is in danger of running out of places to happen.

One answer is to create more places to sail. Many years ago on a rainy afternoon, I settled down with a civil engineer to work out how much it would cost to build an island in the shallow waters off the South Coast to create another Solent.

Obviously, the larger the area being reclaimed, the cheaper the manufactured land became until, eventually, the point was reached where house site values would justify the works. This point came when the island was a lot smaller than the Isle of Wight, but in my design it had more creeks and bays for yachting! The Dutch would have done it before we thought of it and, perhaps, when we stop building over farm land, we might try it as well.

In the meantime, if you are becoming fed up with queuing for a berth for the weekend, it might be worth keeping the boat further from the southern part of Britain, which has the added value of allowing you to discover another sailing area.

Although the travel time to the boat might be greater; paradoxically there may well be more sailing time because potential destinations are less crowded and there is no need to furl the sails early and rush in to find a berth.

THE LAST LIGHTHOUSE KEEPER

Who is looking out from those infamous headlands, now the last lighthouse keeper has gone and all the lights are automated? Yachtsmen may feel a little lonelier, but safety should not be an issue, Robin maintains.

Headlands play an important part in voyages. They are usually the last points from which a navigator can make a departure and often the first recognisable land at his destination.

On coastal voyages headlands mark progress, usually mean an alteration of course, are an easy reference and can often provide shelter on one side or another from unfavourable conditions. In the era of exploration they were frequently a psychological barrier or the last obstacle when opening a new route.

Since they were so important to navigators in the days of sail, their names are distinctive: Land's End, Lizard, Start Point, Portland Bill, South and North Foreland. Some names reflect the look of the headland; others its location.

Start Point presumably got its name from the fact that it was an often used departure point for vessels leaving the United Kingdom on a voyage to the south-west. The Cape of Good Hope was named because it marked the end of a long search for a route around Africa.

Naturally, vessels sailing along a coast tended to sail from headland to headland, which led to losses, particularly when fog or mist came down.

So it is not surprising that, as the number of ships increased, the demand for better identification of headlands grew, and they became second only to port entrances to have lighthouses built on them. As the lights became more sophisticated, they were able to give a clearly discernible identification to the promontory.

Before the days of radio, these lighthouses performed the additional service of acting as reporting stations, advising owners, often via Lloyd's, of the passing of vessels; this was frequently the first news of a safe return from a long voyage.

Of course, the presence of men in the lighthouses who understood and recognised vessels added to their security as a vessel in trouble could be seen and assistance despatched.

So 26 November 1998 saw the end of an era when the North Foreland Lighthouse was automated – the last manned lighthouse in the whole of the United Kingdom and Republic of Ireland.

Its de-manning was inevitable because labour costs had spiralled upwards and, even more relevant, modern equipment had become so reliable that a permanent watchkeeper became quite unnecessary. The new system costs less and is just as reliable, achieving reliability rating in excess of 99.8%.

With the decline in the number of Coastguard stations, there are fewer eyes searching seaward, so from the yachtsman's point of view the loss of the lighthouse keepers has meant a little less security.

Modern science has given us a more than adequate substitute, though, in the form of VHF radio, and the mobile phone is becoming worldwide, providing an additional effective means of calling for help.

Navigation marks are still there – Trinity House alone has 77 light-houses, 11 light vessels and two light floats, and 427 buoys in service – and ports provide many more navigation marks within their own areas. Position-fixing is so much easier and effective nowadays.

Decca gave us a very accurate means of fixing our position and GPS is even more accessible. New computerised charts, interfaced with the GPS, are providing an instant plot, which can be fitted to any cruising or racing yacht.

So, although a yacht crew might feel a little lonelier as they beat around a headland, knowing that no longer is anyone looking down and watching their progress, safety should not really be an issue.

CASTING CLOUDS

Why can't the BBC leave the Shipping Forecast alone? asks Robin. In 2006 they were
even changing the instantly recognisable theme
music. They've obviously never tried to get a
signal in mid-Atlantic.

So the BBC are changing the music that precedes the early morning
forecast. It seems that every time someone in the management
there wants to show they will fearlessly make changes, they pick
on the inoffensive weather forecasts for seamen. It's an easy target.
Everyone who goes to sea needs to know what the weather is likely to
be. It's not a luxury, it's a necessity, but it tends to be treated as a chore
by the BBC.

Changing that rather lovely piece of music does not affect the actual
forecast, of course. Perhaps that is why the BBC felt it was safe to
remove it. But to many of us, perhaps well out at sea, that music
personifies everything that makes us proud of our country and is much

admired by our foreign visitors. The way the tunes from England, Ireland, Scotland and Wales are cleverly mixed together makes us think of home and the wonderful traditions that the four nations have built up over the centuries together. This is particularly true of our maritime traditions, which have always been shared. So why does it have to be changed?

In part, it is because the BBC has never understood the sea or sailing, or the needs of the seafarer. The late John Dunn told me that he was told when he read the forecasts that he could read it through fast as all seafarers had a special form of writing and could take it down quickly.

It was not until he accompanied me to Iceland that he appreciated how important the forecasts are. He suddenly realised we were struggling to write the forecast down in our own form of shorthand and how hard it was to take down when they were read in such a rush. Sadly, he was not able to persuade any of the other readers of this simple fact.

The BBC played with the forecasts some time ago, when the broadcast times were changed. Not the end of the world, but I don't think they understood why it helped seafarers to have forecasts every six hours. Our requirements did not fit into their schedules.

This was the same time they decided to drop the weather forecasts from local stations except for once a day, because, I suppose, it lengthened the time it took to read the forecast. They did not appreciate that a forecast is just that, at best a guess of what the weather might do, while the reports from local stations told us what is really happening. Putting the two together could tell seafarers what the forecasters thought might be coming and where it had reached. This is vital because the weather does not always co-operate with the forecasts, as we all know.

I wrote to the Director General about this, explaining that those extra two minutes giving us the actual conditions were vital, but I was told that the Royal Yachting Association had agreed the change. I found this hard to believe and contacted the RYA. They denied they had ever been asked and had certainly not agreed to the changes. My follow-up letter to the Director General of the BBC asking for a further explanation in view of this information went unanswered.

Changing the tune that precedes the forecast is not the end of the world, but then, why do it? It is easily recognised, which is something that anyone who has tried to tune in a radio when miles out at sea and reception is poor, readily appreciates. Radio waves are funny things. They can be disrupted by distance, change in time of day, sunspots, battery power, you name it; they all contribute to difficulties in reception.

Having something familiar and recognisable helps you to get the best reception. They have probably never tried to pick up a weak signal from halfway across the Atlantic. In fact, with a low-power receiver, 500 miles can create difficulties. If something is working, don't play with it has always been a good maxim, and this example fits the bill perfectly.

So come on, BBC, that tune has worked for years, leave it alone! If you must make changes, just give us back the reports from coastal stations in every forecast. It could save lives and would help towards convincing seafarers that you have some appreciation that we live on an island, and that the sea, and its moods, matter to some five million of us licence payers.

A SEA OF RUBBISH

Forget supermarket bags on the streets, plastic afloat is as damaging to a yacht as it is to the environment, never mind the unsightly mess it makes of our anchorages, says Robin.

There are few sights more depressing than seeing plastic in the sea. The Marpol Treaty has been in force since October 1983, its sole objective to preserve the marine environment through a complete ban on dumping oil and other dangerous substances, including garbage and sewage – basically anything from ships. Yet we still see plastic bags, sheets, bottles and boxes floating around.

From my own observations there seems to be more of it around the coasts than out in the oceans. In fact, there is less rubbish in the oceans than there was 40 years ago, although then there was as much wood as plastic in the water, a good part of it made up of dunnage, the timber planks that were used to separate cargo in the days before containers and which were chucked over the side when ships cleaned their holds. This would tend to indicate that the source of a lot of the plastic we see around our coasts is from the shore. One look at the Thames would tend to confirm this. If it gets into a river it will end up in the sea, where it is unsightly, unpleasant and can be dangerous.

Most sailors tend to be environmentalists because none of us wish to see rubbish floating in our favourite anchorages or when out sailing. In addition, the provision of garbage collection points in ports and marinas means it is fairly convenient to collect your rubbish on board and get rid of it properly when you reach shore.

But this does not deal with the plastic that comes out to sea from the land. The solution lies ashore, but we have to deal with the effects. So I was interested in an idea that was put forward by the Little Ship Club. It proposes that we sailors should pick up plastic rubbish we see floating around and use it as a target for a man overboard drill in the process. This seems to be quite a smart idea to me. We improve our boat-handling skills and tidy up the sea at the same time.

We hear the cry of the environmentalists about jetsam in the sea and the death it can bring to animals – turtles swallowing plastic in the mistaken belief it is jellyfish, dolphins caught in the stuff, fish trapped. All this is damaging and in the end we humans will suffer for it. More instantly inconvenient to the yachtsman is the plastic that gets sucked into an engine intake or trapped around a propeller.

Both can prove quite dangerous. An engine overheating as the boat is manoeuvring in strong winds or tide can mean damage at best, loss of a boat at worst. Even a shopping bag around the prop will reduce performance, but industrial plastic sheeting can jam it completely. If you are lucky the effect will be gradual rather than that heart-wrenching clunk which means that all the torque from the engine has been dumped onto the gear box or engine mountings and an expensive bill is going to follow – once the immediate problem has been sorted out, that is.

On one occasion I was motoring up the Thames and had just drawn level with the Wapping River Police base when my engine ground to a halt. Looking over the side I could see a large sheet of plastic around the propeller. We tried to deal with it from on deck. We tried reversing the engine. No good. Because we were drifting at four knots we dropped the anchor. The tide was flooding fast. The anchor, a CQR, did not hold on the smooth gravel bottom. We put out all the 22 fathoms of chain I carried, but we were still dragging upriver and Tower Bridge was coming into sight. The thought of being swept onto the bridge where the masts would catch galvanised me into action.

I removed my clothes and jumped into the water. It took less than a minute to clear the prop once I was on top of the job and I climbed back on board. As I did so I became aware of a river police launch almost alongside. They had seen our plight and come out to offer assistance.

The coxswain was a lady and conscious of my nakedness I grabbed a towel to maintain some measure of dignity. She had probably seen worse – or better – sights before. However, she would have been spared the view altogether if that piece of plastic had not been floating in the river.

INDEX